THE ECONOMIC DEVELOPMENT OF *Kuwait*

Report of Missions Organized by the
International Bank for Reconstruction and Development
at the Request of
the Government of Kuwait

THE ECONOMIC DEVELOPMENT

OF KUWAIT

PUBLISHED FOR The International Bank for Reconstruction and Development
BY The Johns Hopkins Press, Baltimore

1961

Syed Amjad Ali,	Chief of Mission
O. J. McDiarmid,	Chief Economist
Glen Brown,	Water Resources
John Derrick,	Industry
Harold Holtz,	Public Works
Abdul H. Kadhim,	Education
J. H. Van Mook,	Public Administration
Carl Murray,	Budget and Fiscal Accounting
Anders Ølgaard,	Industrial Economist
George Ponghis,	Public Health

1963

O. J. McDiarmid,	Chief of Mission
Jean Baneth,	Economist
John Derrick,	Industrial Adviser

The oil resources of Kuwait, about one-fifth of the world total, give the Sheikhdom a much larger role in the economic affairs of the Middle East than its modest geographical dimensions and population might indicate. Alone among countries of the region, Kuwait has been able to pursue vigorous internal development while exporting capital in important amounts. Through the Kuwait Fund for Arab Economic Development and a grant aid program to neighboring countries, Kuwait is beginning to make a significant contribution toward meeting the capital needs of the Arab World, including several North African countries.

The lack of physical resources other than oil, and particularly the great scarcity of water, presents a real challenge to the Government in its endeavor to use its oil revenues more productively at home as well as abroad. It is now endeavoring to broaden the pattern of internal investment beyond the construction of social capital assets, private housing and commercial structures on which most past capital expenditures have concentrated.

The need for further consideration of its internal goals and programs prompted the Government to ask the Bank to send an Economic Mission to Kuwait in March 1961 to prepare a report for the Government. The Mission had comprehensive terms of reference. The Government desired assistance in improving public administration as well as help in formulating its future health, education and investment programs. The social services of the State, particularly in education and health, are on a par with those in well developed countries. The use of hydrocarbon resources required special investigation, since any broadening of the pattern of internal investments is likely to involve industries based on these resources. The examination of water prospects also was given close attention.

The Bank was fortunate in receiving the cooperation of the United Nations and the specialized agencies in recruiting the Mission. WHO and UNESCO made staff members available as public health and education advisers, and the United Nations also was instrumental in helping the Bank obtain the services of public administration and budget and accounting experts. The United States Government lent the Mission an adviser on water resources.

The Mission received excellent support from the government personnel assigned to work with it in Kuwait. The Presidents of the various government departments, the Directors General and other responsible officials were generous in giving their time and advice and in complying with the Mission's requests for information. His Excellency Sheikh Jabir Al-Ahmad Al-Sabah, President of the then Department of Finance and Economy, who initiated the request for the Mission, gave it especially valuable guidance and support. The Kuwait Chamber of Commerce, officials of the private banks and other leaders of the business community provided significant data and advice. The thanks of the Mission are also due to the Political Agency of the United Kingdom and to the American Consulate, the two foreign government missions in Kuwait at the time of the Mission's visit.

In 1963, at the invitation of the Government, a small Mission visited Kuwait to bring up to date the 1961 report. The following report was prepared by that Mission. At the request of the Government, wherever possible this report contains the recommendations that were made by the 1961 Mission and refers to the action that has since been taken to carry them out. The members of the 1961 Mission have not reviewed this report, however, and are not responsible for its content.

CONTENTS

CHAPTER 1 *SUMMARY OF THE REPORT*

The Economy

Kuwait's oil constitutes a huge and only very gradually diminishing stock of capital. At current rates of production, reserves appear ample for 80 to 100 years. Therefore, assuming no technological revolution which would make petroleum an obsolete commodity, the major support for the Kuwait economy will long be its petroleum resources.

Diversification and more broadly based employment opportunities may be achieved by more internal investment of the financial resources derived from oil and by using natural gas and other hydrocarbons for power and industrial raw materials. This will not substantially alter the dependence of the economy on petroleum. However, the Government is wise in taking thought for the time when oil exports may be less remunerative and other sources of income will be welcome. Also, regardless of purely income considerations, a more diversified economy providing a wider range of occupations for the people would make for a better and more attractive social environment in Kuwait.

Indeed, Kuwait has reached the level of affluence where purely economic improvement, in the form of a higher per capita income for her people, need not be an overriding objective of national policy. She is almost uniquely capable of rapid internal development while contributing to the economic, educational and health programs of less fortunate countries. The need for improvement of life in Kuwait and the possibility of benefits from further expansion of the assistance Kuwait is already providing other countries, particularly in the Middle East, influenced many of the recommendations in this report. Domestic needs and investment opportunities were given priority in our thinking but not to the point of proposing uneconomic or wasteful projects in Kuwait such as industrial ventures which would have to rely on heavy subsidies or trade restrictions.

The Government realizes the heavy responsibility it has for making the best use of those public funds which it decides to use for investment purposes. The Mission's recommendations concerning the amount and allocation of such funds are contained in Chapter 6.

In preparing its suggestions on this subject, the Mission was, of course, confronted with a different set of problems from those encountered in countries of limited financial, but more diversified physical and human resources. For all practical purposes Kuwait

1

has no natural physical resources except petroleum, natural gas and easy access to the sea. However, on the human resources side, the business talent of the Kuwaiti stock, long familiar with maritime life and commerce, has been combined in recent years with the technical skill and energy of a diversified and generally capable expatriate community. Non-Kuwaiti residents make up at least half the population and two-thirds of the work force, including nearly all those with professional training. The immigration of these workers to Kuwait, largely without their families, was mainly responsible for the phenomenally rapid growth of population by an estimated 10–12 per cent a year from 1957 to 1961. The 1961 census recorded 321,000 residents, and (allowing for some who probably were not counted in 1961) the population probably approximates 350,000 or more today.

The oil industry in Kuwait is, of course, not hampered by the small market, high labor cost and lack of raw material that handicap the establishment of other industries. It is indeed of unparalleled efficiency, with unit costs well below those of other Middle East producers. Commercial exploitation started after World War II, and production now exceeds 100 million metric tons a year, making Kuwait second only to Venezuela as an oil exporter and fourth among the world's crude producers. The economy of the State is based almost completely on the oil revenues. They probably exceeded a half billion dollars in 1963/64,[1] or about $1,450 per capita. This income has been increasing on the average at about 8 per cent annually in recent years.

The revenues from oil and income from foreign investment accumulated from past oil receipts are the only significant source of budgetary income for the Government and of foreign exchange for the country. Roughly half the foreign exchange income from the oil sector (including the local expenditures of the oil companies) in 1962/63 was used for commodity imports retained in Kuwait, about 18 per cent was invested abroad by the Government and about 32 per cent was used either for foreign private investment or otherwise remitted abroad by the private sector (including immigrant or expatriate remittances). Earnings from the Government's foreign assets, the only other known foreign exchange earnings of any consequence (nearly all commodity exports are re-exports), were reinvested abroad.

The Bank Mission that visited Kuwait in 1961 estimated the Sheikhdom's 1959 Gross National Product (excluding the retained

[1] The Kuwait fiscal year is from April 1 to March 31.

earnings of the foreign oil companies) at about 296 million Kuwait dinars ($828 million) or about $3,200 per capita. A similar estimate for 1962/63 is KD 370 million ($1,057 million) indicating a growth of about 8 per cent a year.[2] Because of the sharp increase in population during the intervening years, the present per capita GNP (estimated at $2,960) is probably somewhat lower than in 1959 though it is probably still the highest in the world. Since from 40–50 per cent of both public and private income is saved, consumption levels, though high, are by no means proportionate to per capita income.

The very high rate of savings, together with the fact that about half of GNP is in foreign exchange, has made it possible for Kuwait to maintain an open economy for imports and financial remittances. Thus external rather than domestic influences have determined prices and, to some extent, interest rates in Kuwait. However, labor has commanded much higher wages in Kuwait than in surrounding countries. The high wage policy of the Government, which employs about a third of the labor force, has artificially raised the wage structure throughout the economy. Also, skilled labor is not easily attracted to the somewhat austere living conditions of Kuwait.

Investment in the Public Sector

The 1961 Bank Mission recommended to the Government that 28 per cent of the total revenues of the State be used for domestic development expenditures. This would have involved an average annual outlay of about KD 57 million, KD 44 million in the public sector and KD 13 million of public investment in industrial projects in, or in association with, the private sector. In fact, actual expenditures for public works in 1961/62 and 1962/63 were about KD 35 million a year (19 per cent of total public revenues as compared with the 22 per cent suggested by the Mission), and investment of public funds in the private sector (which was expected to absorb 6 per cent of public revenues) scarcely got under way until recently. The gap that this curtailment of public investment made in the flow of funds to the private sector was compensated for by large-scale purchases of land by the State and by some increase in current expenditures.

The Mission recognized that the level of business activity in Kuwait, under present circumstances, largely depends on the flow of public

[2] See Appendix 1 for details of these estimates.

funds to the private sector. Therefore its recommendations contemplated that the level of total expenditures in the Kuwait economy
during the next five years should be maintained at about the 1960/61
level. However, it suggested that the purchase of land by the Government should be reduced to about 30 per cent of the 1960/61
level by 1963/64.

The Government buys land at highly inflated prices for development projects and for resale to private buyers. Land purchases
amounted to between KD 40 million and KD 60 million in most recent
years. Whatever the political or developmental justifications for this
practice, the prices fixed by the Government for these transactions and
the small amount thus far collected on the resale of the land make the
public land transactions a rather indiscriminate and inequitable way
of distributing the oil revenues. In addition, probably the largest
share of these funds are invested abroad, so that the land purchase
program fails to accomplish its main objective of invigorating the
Kuwait economy. The Mission therefore proposed that this method
of disbursing public funds to the private sector should be in part
replaced by government investment in private or quasi-private industry and in part by increased capital expenditures on public works.
The Mission hoped that the income-generating expenditures required
for the growth of the economy would come largely from increased
private investment and the expansion of the private and quasi-private
sectors.

Although the Government has, partly by force of circumstances
(including the crisis with Iraq), followed a different course (increasing
current expenditures and land purchases), the expenditure pattern
suggested by the 1961 Mission still appears sound. Thus, in 1961/62
and 1962/63 the Government spent for public works about 80 per cent
of the amount recommended by the 1961 Mission. The amount
budgeted in 1963/64 for expenditure on public works, however, is
58 per cent above the average of the previous two years; and if the
total expenditure contemplated through 1965/66 is actually made, the
public investments during the five-year period 1961/62–1965/66 may
approximate the level recommended by the 1961 Mission, or about
KD 200 million. There will, however, likely be some shortfall in actual
as compared with budgeted expenditures as in the past.

The 1963 Bank Mission did not attempt to project outlays beyond
1965/66, since the newly organized Planning Board intends to prepare a five-year plan starting at about that time. Although individual
projects such as the seaport, the airport and the road network have

been planned and engineered with care, there as yet has been no coordinated phasing of the different projects nor even realistic projections of total development expenditures for more than one year. The 1961 Mission recommended the establishment of a Planning or Development Board at ministerial level for this purpose. A Planning Board has now been established with the Prime Minister as Chairman. It has even more extensive powers than the Bank Mission had suggested. When it has recruited an adequate technical staff (which is now being done), it should supply an urgently needed focal point of economic coordination, research and planning.

Housing and water supply are two fields in which more funds could profitably be spent than in the past. A low income housing program has been started, but it seems to be moving fairly slowly. Chapter 7 of this report suggests some modification in the program, particularly the broadening of its coverage to include deserving non-Kuwaiti families. Water is, of course, the most important lack of Kuwait, yet we feel that the search for usable water is not being pressed very energetically. Distilled water and a limited supply of fresh water are already available, albeit at a high price, for normal municipal purposes. The main problem is to try to obtain at least a limited amount for irrigation for growing fresh vegetables and in order to make Kuwait a more attractive place in which to live. Perhaps a usable underground water supply can be discovered in the southwest corner of the country (which the 1961 Mission thought possible) or water can be piped from the Shatt-al-Arab River in Iraq. Economically the latter scheme seems entirely feasible and plans are being made to carry it out.

Development of the Private Sector

Import trade and merchandising, construction and personal service occupations have naturally dominated economic activities in the private sector during the last 12 years. The traditional occupations of seaborne trade, boat building, fishing and pearling, all rather labor intensive in character, have declined to relative insignificance because much higher incomes could be obtained more easily in other ways. The high wage structure in the government services and the oil sector, together with the lack of raw materials and water, has made industrial investment relatively unattractive despite the high level of private savings and abundance of cheap capital.

Despite these circumstances a number of small industries have been established, mostly to produce construction materials, the marketing of which is favored both by the comparatively high cost of importing materials and large consumption by the Government. It is not surprising, therefore, that direct government participation in the ownership and control of industry has been one of the principal incentives for private investment. It seemed to the 1961 Mission that public participation and control of industries selling to the Government could easily lead either to disagreement on policy questions between the public and the private representatives on the boards of directors or to an undesirable conflict of interest between the Government as seller and buyer of the same products. Besides, in Kuwait there should be no shortage either of venture capital or management capacity in the private sector. In those cases where the Government wished to underwrite some of the risks connected with the establishment of new industries it could do so by extending long-term, low-interest loans through its medium and long-term lending institution, the Credit Bank. This observation does not apply, however, to large-scale investment in petrochemicals and possibly metallurgical industries, where the equity involved would be too large for the private sector to absorb, at least in the short run.

The two Bank Missions have given much thought to the role that the Government might play in encouraging the establishment of private industries in Kuwait. It could do this either by positive steps such as providing low-cost capital and technical assistance or by negative measures such as imposing high tariffs and import restrictions. These are matters on which Kuwaiti officials and businessmen seem to be quite divided. We have concluded that there are some cogent reasons for positive measures of the first sort, but we would not favor restrictive action along the latter line except for very modest import duties on a temporary basis.

Our reasons may be summarized as follows:

a) With its abundance of capital and hydrocarbon raw materials plus good shipping facilities, Kuwait should be competitive in capital-intensive petrochemical industries, provided good export connections are established.

b) There are a large number of workers on the public payroll. Although highly paid by Middle East standards, these workers are unproductive in their present occupations. The transfer of selected groups to jobs in industry, even if special incentives, including subsidies, were necessary to establish the industries, would certainly increase the national product of the country.

Such incentives, provided the industries are not uneconomic on grounds other than labor costs, therefore, should be regarded sympathetically by the Government. It is realized, of course, that even the best of these people would require training to fit them for industrial jobs.

c) While Kuwait's population is small, the level of imports is comparable to that of a sizable, but lower income country. Therefore, lack of a market is not a reason for denying that possibilities exist for producing at a profit selected items such as glass, tires, paint, batteries, and so forth.[3]

We realize that, while Kuwait's comparative advantage lies mainly in certain capital-intensive industries (e.g., petrochemicals), the argument most frequently heard for special incentives or protection for industry is that a means must be found to employ the labor that will be surplus when construction activity declines. A recent report estimated that, for the industries which might be competitive in Kuwait or which could get along with reasonable tariffs only, an investment of nearly KD 21 million would be required to employ 1,200 workers.[4] Since there are probably from 20,000 to 25,000 construction workers now employed, new industries are not a substitute for this activity which, in any event, is likely to continue for quite a long time. Therefore, we feel that though some new industries are possible, they will not be a substitute for the construction industry or the government as employers of labor.

The following incentives might be provided for the establishment of private industries:

a) Imports of raw materials, machinery and spare parts should be exempted from the 4 per cent *ad valorem* duty.

b) The Government should build an industrial estate and be liberal in providing required offsite facilities such as workers' housing and public utilities. The initial capital costs should be borne by the Government and amortized out of charges over long periods and at low rates of interest.

c) The Government should be prepared to incur the capital costs involved in installing additional power and water production facilities for industrial use outside the proposed industrial

[3] See Chapter 8.
[4] *Industrial and Process Engineering Consultants: Industrial Survey (of Kuwait)*— 1963.

estate. The Mission would not recommend, however, that rates charged for power and water produced in government-owned facilities be lower than the prime operating costs of such facilities.

d) The advisory and technical services of the Government Credit Bank (then being created) should be made available in the establishment of new industry. The Bank should be liberal in making such services available even when it is not participating financially in the enterprise.

Since 1961 the Government has proceeded with plans for an industrial estate for larger-scale industries. It has also entered into an agreement with British Petroleum and Gulf Oil, the two partners in the Kuwait Oil Company (KOC), for the manufacture of fertilizers from natural gas. When the 1963 Mission was in Kuwait a "Law for the Regulation, Protection and Encouragement of Industry" was being considered. The draft law provided for import restrictions, tariffs and licensing to control entry of competitors, in addition to the type of incentives recommended above. We suggest that import restrictions and licensing are not desirable and that only moderate tariffs for a limited period should be considered.[5]

Allocation of Financial Resources

Kuwait is expected to receive as oil revenues and other public income about KD 660 million in the three years 1963/64 through 1965/66. The 1963 Mission expects current expenditures to require about KD 260 million, or about the same proportion of total revenues as in recent years. This will leave KD 400 million for investment and for transfer to the private sector. The investment program in the public sector should require not more than KD 120 million, with major emphasis on completing public works projects now under way, more housing, expanded water and power facilities and a start toward an adequate telephone system. In addition, the Government should spend about KD 50 million on an industrial estate and projects for the utilization of its natural gas resources in which private foreign capital will participate. The remaining KD 230 million will be divided between foreign investments and transfers to the private sector through the medium of land purchases in Kuwait.

[5] See Chapter 8.

The 1963 Mission, like its predecessor, recommends that expenditures for land purchases be substantially reduced. However, for the development of the remaining "old city" of Kuwait purchases of about KD 20 million a year will be necessary. Taking into account the fact that the Government recently has been purchasing a large amount of land to be paid for over a period of years, it may not be able to reduce its outlays below a total of KD 80 million over the next three years. (At the same time it is strongly recommended that the amount received from the resale of land to the private sector be sharply increased above its present quite nominal amount.) This would leave KD 150 million for foreign investment. Public disbursements in Kuwait would be maintained at their 1962/63 level of about KD 160 million a year.

Kuwait has made striking progress since 1961 in placing the management of its foreign investments on a sound basis. The Kuwait Fund for Arab Economic Development, capitalized at KD 100 million, is already contributing substantially to the progress of a number of countries. Its loans total KD 20.4 million, and several more are under consideration. It is equipped with a competent professional staff. Fortunately, the Government has seen the wisdom of maintaining the independence of the Fund from political influences. Non-project loans (notably KD 30 million made recently to Iraq) are not channeled through the Fund. Also, since 1961, the Government has sought advice from distinguished experts on the management of its revenue-yielding foreign investments in the United Kingdom and elsewhere.

Other Economic Policies

Tax Policy. At present the only tax levied on the domestic economy is a 4 per cent *ad valorem* duty on foreign trade. The income tax law is intended to apply only to the foreign participations in business in Kuwait. A rate of 50 per cent applies on the total net income of the business when such net income exceeds about KD 375,000. Just how this will be applied in the case of partly foreign and partly Kuwaiti-owned enterprises is uncertain. At present, taxes are collected only on wholly foreign-owned enterprises. The Mission feels that such a high rate at this relatively low level of net income and the discrimination against foreign investments are discouraging to the latter. It also believes that since the tax applies only to the return on equity and not to interest paid on loans, it may lead to an undue portion of financing from abroad being offered on a loan basis, thus distorting the financial structure of joint Kuwaiti-foreign companies by encouraging too high a debt-equity ratio.

Kuwait has abundant capital resources both in the public and private sectors, and at the present time does not feel a pressing need to provide new job opportunities. But the Government does not require taxes for fiscal reasons; it is anxious to broaden the economic base, and is entertaining proposals for complex new industries which cannot be established without foreign participation and technical and managerial assistance. Despite the wealth of the economy during the last decade, a comparatively small amount of industrial investment has been made by Kuwaitis. Consequently, the Mission suggests that the Government either raise the amount of net income to which the maximum rate applies or considerably reduce the maximum tax rate. The Mission does not believe that the return on capital likely to be earned by companies in Kuwait producing for the export market, which are those in which foreign investors are likely to be interested, will be so high as to make this proposed reduction in the income tax unreasonable. The Mission is aware of the need for avoiding any prejudice to the present profit-sharing formula with the oil companies. But there seems no reason why a mutually agreeable arrangement could not be worked out with the companies which would give the Government latitude in adjusting income tax rates applicable to other foreign investments in Kuwait.

In view of the abundance of public income, the Mission does not think it necessary to propose a tax program for Kuwait. If additional revenues are needed later, a levy on the capital value of land, or better on the capital gains obtained from transactions in land, would be justified. Under the present circumstances the Mission believes that the public utilities should pay their way (aside from the possible explicit subsidy for industry mentioned above), so as not to distort the price structure unduly and not to subsidize mainly those most able to pay. Registration fees for motor vehicles should also be increased from their present nominal amounts in view of the benefits derived from the large capital expenditures on roads. We also suggest that the port charges which are now extremely low should be increased so as to cover current expenditures on the Port.

Central Bank. The establishment of a central bank to replace the Currency Board is under consideration. Kuwait does not seem to require many of the usual services of a central bank. From the standpoint of credit control, the liquidity of the commercial banks is now extremely high, but their lending policies are quite conservative.

They appear to meet the legitimate credit needs of the economy. It is very doubtful whether a central bank would be particularly well placed to provide extensive services as fiscal adviser to the Government, since the Government does not have to concern itself either with an internal or an external public debt. A very useful service which a central bank might perform is in the field of research and statistics. The Mission is glad to note that the Currency Board is gathering monetary statistics for Kuwait on a regular basis. However, no agency is concerning itself with balance of payments estimates or any sort of national accounts compilation. This would be an appropriate field for the research department of a central bank.

Statistics. The 1961 Mission observed that almost all statistical data needed to prepare an economic report on Kuwait had to be obtained on an *ad hoc* and largely confidential basis. Fortunately this situation has now improved. Up-to-date information on the public finances, prices, wages, employment and production of Kuwait, however, are still very difficult to obtain. We hope that periodic reports on all aspects of the economy will soon be prepared and published by the Central Statistical Office in the Planning Board. This would do much to eliminate some misconceptions of Kuwait that are still widely held abroad.

Foreign Participation. Certain features of the Commercial Code (Amiri Decree 15 of 1960) discriminate strongly against foreign business activity in Kuwait. Some, such as the requirement of at least 51 per cent national ownership of all business organizations, while not conducive to encouraging private investment are, nevertheless, frequently found in commercial codes of other countries. The requirement that a Kuwaiti partner with a controlling voice should be obtained by all foreigners seeking to do business in Kuwait, however, and the total exclusion of foreigners from entering into new insurance and banking ventures, go considerably beyond the usual practice, and in the opinion of the Mission should be altered. If, as we believe would be desirable, Kuwait wishes to expand abroad in the fields of banking and insurance, it will have to grant reciprocity by allowing foreign establishments to operate in Kuwait.

Naturalization Policy. The level, composition and rate of growth of a country's population are certainly among the most basic determinants of its economic development. Insofar as the Mission could ascertain, the authorities have not yet formulated a positive policy respecting the number and composition of the future population of the State. As we note in Chapter 2, the present naturalization laws are very restrictive, though the construction of public works and the rest of the social capital of the country, as well as the commercial part of the private sector, is geared to the present population of Kuwait plus a fairly rapid growth in the future. It is beyond the terms of reference of the Mission to make a recommendation on the broad subject of population policy, but we strongly urge the Government to give it careful attention. From the standpoint of the economy's stability and growth, we believe that the country's best interests would be served by liberalizing its naturalization policy, particularly to give citizenship to all children born in Kuwait after they have resided there for a reasonable period, and to liberalize naturalization restrictions on expatriates who are capable of contributing substantially to the economy.

Public Administration

In June 1961, a new treaty with the United Kingdom gave Kuwait full control over her foreign relations, which since 1899 had been handled through the British Foreign Office. Since that time Kuwait has been moving rapidly toward representative government. A constitution has been promulgated and a National Assembly elected to which the ministers of the government (except the Prime Minister) are responsible, though they continue to be appointed by the Ruler. In view of these developments, several of the recommendations of the 1961 Bank Mission on the central government structure have been overtaken by events. For example, that Mission recommended that a Chairman of the Supreme Council be appointed, and that he have directly under him various functions required for the better coordination of the Government. The new constitution provides for a Prime Minister who in fact performs most of the functions that the Mission had envisaged for the Chairman of the Supreme Council. He presides over its successor body, the Council of Ministers, and over the Planning Board which has been established along lines recommended by the Mission. Other innovations suggested, such as an independent auditor general and civil service commission reporting directly to the top echelons in the Government, have been accepted in principle.

However, at the ministerial or department level there still exists no organizational decree establishing the functions of the different ministries, nor is there any agency responsible for studying this matter on a continuing basis. Since some overlapping of responsibilities continues to exist, we repeat the recommendation in the 1961 report that a committee be established under the Council of Ministers to consider and recommend reforms in the organization of the Executive Branch of the Government.

Since the number of ministries has been reduced from 19 to 14 (the 1961 Mission had suggested 12), considerable progress has been made in simplifying the executive and administrative machinery. The 1961 Mission had also suggested that the State-wide functions of the Municipality Department be merged with responsibilities for natural resources and agriculture, located elsewhere in the Government, and that a new Ministry of Interior and Municipality be established. This still appears to be desirable, although since a Ministry of Interior has been established with largely police duties, a name such as Natural Resources and Municipality Ministry might now be more appropriate.

Probably the two fields which are still most in need of attention at the administrative level are the management of the civil service and fiscal accounting and controls. The Civil Service Regulations *per se* appear to be generally satisfactory, but they allow sweeping exceptions regarding qualifications for appointment, grading, and similar vital matters. The result is that political considerations, including personal relationships, often outweigh merit in obtaining a government job or advancing to a better position. There are many unqualified employees, and general standards of education and performance are low. Redundancy of personnel is the rule in many public agencies. The closing of loopholes in the Regulations combined with a training program as suggested in this report are strongly recommended.

In respect of budget and accounting, the present reasonably satisfactory budget law should be enforced. The review of the annual capital budgets by the Planning Board is a useful exercise. The disbursement of public funds is not well controlled, however, and fiscal accounting needs fundamental improvement and unification. The 1963 Bank Mission was glad to note that two suggestions of the previous Mission, namely, the centralization of disbursement in the Ministry of Finance and Industry, and the appointment of an auditor general had been accepted in principle and would be carried out as soon as possible.

Public Health

All health services, including the most modern hospitalization, are free in Kuwait to residents and non-residents alike. Both in terms of physical facilities and medical personnel, the State ranks among the best equipped countries in the world. The Ministry of Public Health is doing a very commendable job. However, as in most new public health services, greater emphasis has been placed on curative than on preventive medicine. Strengthening of preventive medicine is now most desirable. Special mention should be made of tuberculosis control, which has already been the subject of study and recommendations by an expert of WHO. Tuberculosis control in all its aspects should be united under the Tuberculosis Division of the Ministry of Health, which should be closely coordinated with, and provide technical guidance and supervision to, all health units in the country giving anti-tuberculosis services. Trachoma is another disease requiring special attention. It is said to be widespread but mild in Kuwait City but more severe in the villages. A central program should be developed. Similar attention should be given to the maternal and child welfare activities, where preventive medicine again needs reinforcement and extension. An expert in this field to study the conditions and needs and make the necessary recommendations is advisable. With the development and strengthening of preventive medicine, a more adequate public health laboratory should be provided.

A serious health problem arises in Kuwait because the population is constantly being increased by an influx of people from the neighboring countries, many bearing diseases. In the words of the Health Ministry, "Until a perfect plan is worked out to put a limit to these uncontrolled movements of population, a great burden is put on the preventive medicine section, and it is very difficult for this department to achieve the perfection it is hoping for." Better immigration control seems to be the only answer to this problem, to assure that those requiring treatment are isolated from the rest of the population.

Vital and health statistics should be greatly improved. Statistics provide the material on which planning, programing and evaluation is done. The need to improve and expand this service is recognized. Even with a Central Statistical Office there will still be the need for a specialized statistical unit in the Public Health Ministry. Even the proper registration of births and deaths, particularly the latter, is neglected. More serious is the failure to keep reliable statistics on the incidence of communicable diseases.

More and more Kuwait is shifting from a natural environment to a man-made one. The problem regarding environmental sanitation cannot but be influenced by this development, and it is necessary to give special attention to the service which should deal with them. The importance of such a service is further enhanced by the fact that several departments have a say and a share in the shaping of the environment, and there is a definite need for the Ministry of Public Health to assume its responsibility regarding the health implications of these developments.

Basic responsibilities which are generally recognized as belonging to health should be assigned to health personnel. Veterinary services and insect control, while administratively under the jurisdiction of other departments, should be supervised by persons acceptable to the Ministry of Health, and procedures used should be reviewed and approved by that Ministry. Also, sanitary arrangements in respect to the handling and distribution of food should be the responsibility of that Ministry rather than the Municipality.

Water supply is, of course, a particularly difficult problem in Kuwait. Route sampling and chemical examinations almost always show that chlorine added at the distillation plant is completely exhausted by the rusted pipes and sulphur and iron bacteria. Until the present piping system is corrected, the installation of secondary chlorinators at the distribution stations is recommended. A recent school health survey has shown that school children have approximately two decayed, missing or filled teeth per student. The problem is growing and the only reasonable solution is the fluoridation of the water supply.

The rapid development of the City of Kuwait should not increase the existing differences between village and urban life. On the contrary, parallel development should be undertaken outside the city area in order to bring economic, social and cultural improvement and prevent the problems that an unbalanced development might create. In this connection, the elimination of the existing slums should be among the first programs to be undertaken.

The problem of health personnel is also an important one. It is true that Kuwait can afford to import all the personnel required, but there are some difficulties: first in getting the personnel of the training and experience needed, second in using persons of various backgrounds, and third, in appointing them for relatively long periods. Ultimately, nationals should be prepared to take over many more jobs and responsibilities. The existing program of fellowships for medical study abroad should be further developed.

Education

Great emphasis is placed in Kuwait on providing the best possible educational facilities through the secondary school level, in both academic and vocational subjects. The school population has grown at a phenomenal rate, and now numbers over 70,000, or about 20 per cent of the total population. A weakness is in technical education, which does not seem to have sufficient appeal although liberal incentives are given to attract students. There are teacher training schools for both men and women although at present about 95 per cent of the Kuwait teaching staff are expatriates.

Since the older members of the community grew up before the oil era made fine and abundant educational facilities possible, there is a large field for adult education which could be cultivated more intensively. At the other end of the education spectrum the question of whether or not to establish a university was and is being debated vigorously.

The following are some important issues:

1) The school curricula should be revised with a view to relating them more closely to the needs and conditions of life in Kuwait. At present they are largely drawn from those of the UAR. Various suggestions are made in this report.

2) Some new school buildings are needed, but the present building program might be extended over a period longer than three years. New school buildings could well be constructed along less elaborate and more functional lines than existing structures.

3) Better selection should be made of students sent abroad at State expense for higher education, to make sure they are productive on their return. We understand that the screening is more thorough than in the past but that the proportion of failures in the course of foreign studies is still high. Students interested in teaching, and with suitable qualifications, should be given a preference in foreign training.

4) Planning for the university should proceed. A start might be made by the establishment of a number of specialized colleges or faculties and research institutes rather than a complete university.

5) Adult education, particularly for women, should be increased.

6) Teacher training and technical and vocational education are the most important fields for emphasis.

The 1963 Mission was glad to note that on such points as stress on in-service teacher training, relief of school supervisors from a heavy burden of administrative duties, and more science in the curriculum, action had been taken along lines recommended in the 1961 report.

CHAPTER **2** *THE STATE*

Geographical and Historical Settings

Kuwait [1] is situated on the northwestern shore of the Persian Gulf, being the most northerly, the largest and the most populous of the Arab Sheikhdoms and communities of the area. It is bounded on the east by the Gulf, on the north and west by Iraq and on the southwest by Saudi Arabia. To the south, Kuwait and Saudi Arabia jointly own the Neutral Zone which also borders the Gulf. The area of the State proper is approximately 6,000 square miles, or somewhat less than that of New Jersey or Wales. The country is roughly rectangular in shape, 130 miles East to West and with a maximum North-South dimension of about 115 miles. The Neutral Zone has an area of about 2,000 square miles. The State includes a number of off-shore islands, the larger of which are Bubiyan, Failakah and Warbah. Only Failakah, the site of an ancient Greek temple built by Alexander's forces, is permanently inhabited. Kuwait Bay is the only prominent coastal feature. It indents the shoreline about 25 miles and provides protection for the port of Kuwait. Half the shoreline of the country lies on Kuwait Bay. Kuwait City and its immediate environs, plus the oil town of Ahmadi and adjacent Fahaheel a few miles to the south, contain all but a few thousand of the State's population, now probably over 350,000. Apart from a small Bedouin population and oil field workers, the Neutral Zone is uninhabited.

Kuwait grew from a settlement on the site of Kuwait City about the beginning of the 18th century, when a number of families of the Anaiza tribe migrated from the interior to the shore of the Gulf. The ruling families of Kuwait, Saudi Arabia and Bahrain stem from this tribe. In 1756 the head of the Al-Sabah family was selected Amir, or Ruler. The need for security and for representation in dealings with the Ottoman Government probably prompted the selection of a leader. An Al-Sabah has been Ruler of Kuwait since that time.

Relations with the British began as a result of the transfer by the East India Company of the southern terminal of its overland mail route (through Aleppo) from Basrah to Kuwait when the former was captured by the Persians during the Turkish-Persian war of 1776.

---

[1] The name of the country is derived from the Arabic diminutive of the word "kut" meaning fort.

The need for protection against raids from the interior encouraged the continuance of these relations, as did the interest of the East India Company in protecting its trade route to India. In 1899 the Ruler, Sheikh Mubarak the Great, sought British protection, which was granted under a treaty similar to those Britain made with other Gulf Sheikhdoms in the 1890s. The Ruler agreed not to cede territory to, or to have direct relations with another power without Britain's consent. Under the treaty the Sheikhdom's foreign relations were handled through the British Foreign Office. In 1904 the British Political Agency was established. Among its other functions it conducted a law court for non-Moslems in the Sheikhdom. The Agency was the only foreign government post in Kuwait until an American Consulate was opened shortly after World War II. In 1914, the British formally agreed that Kuwait was an independent principality under British protection. In 1922, following a brief conflict with Saudi Arabia, and with British assistance, the boundaries of Kuwait were drawn and the Neutral Zone, an area then suspected of containing oil, was established. Fortunately for Kuwait, the southward curve of the boundary with the Neutral Zone was drawn so that the world's richest oil field, the Burgan, all lies in Kuwait.

Governmental power, though vested in the Ruler and his family, derived its main support until the end of World War II from the Kuwaiti merchant families which were the sources of the Sheikhdom's modest prosperity and contributed, directly or indirectly, the major part of its limited government revenue. Foreigners came to the town, but as yet in relatively small numbers. The government structure was simple and lacked the precise division of functions characterizing modern administrations. Actual authority and influence depended greatly on personality, especially that of the Ruler, his nearest relatives and their confidants.

After World War II the material needs of oil exploration and oil production and the feverish development of governmental and private activities in the fields of construction, transport, banking, trade and public services caused a stream of immigration, mainly from Arab countries. The immigrants provided the community with the necessary extra labor, skilled and unskilled, and with the indispensable help of professional people and technicians. As the government income rose by leaps and bounds, to manage it and to put it to proper use, new policies, institutions and government agencies had to be created almost overnight. Distinctions such as those between the privy purse (the civil list) and the public budget, between rule by families and their dependents and government through a civil service, between traditional consultation and elective councils, were hard to grasp and still harder to realize in the turmoil of construction and reorganization. It is indeed striking how much has been achieved under such hectic circumstances and in a very short period.

In the 1950's the primary source of prosperity shifted from the merchants to the Government, which dispensed the oil revenues. Thus the ruling family, and particularly its head, the Ruler, became more important. How these circumstances have influenced public administration in recent years will be discussed in Chapter 3.

In January 1961, the Government announced that Kuwait was now fully responsible for her foreign relations. In June 1961, the 1899 agreement was replaced by a treaty of friendship and consultation with the United Kingdom. The Political Agency's court was abolished. Kuwait has since joined the Arab League, the United Nations and other international agencies. Britain and the United States have established embassies, replacing the Political Agency and the former American Consulate. Diplomatic relations have also been established with a number of other countries, particularly in Asia. Kuwait's international contacts and influence are growing steadily.

Since the new treaty with Britain, Kuwait has been moving rapidly toward democratic government. A constitution has been promulgated and a National Assembly elected to which the ministers heading the various ministries of the Government are responsible, although they continue to be appointed by the Ruler.

Physical Features

Kuwait's climate and physical aspect are, of course, typical of the region. Mean annual rainfall is 4 to 5 inches and average daytime summer temperatures well exceed 110°F. The entire area is semi-arid to arid. There are no springs or streams on the surface. Scarcity of fresh water is thus the major physical problem. The only usable water, in addition to that distilled from the sea, is found trapped in subsurface sedimentary beds. Most of this ground water is brackish to very salty, and is unsuitable for drinking and normal irrigation. When there is good drainage, brackish water is used for the limited irrigation now practiced, but some form of periodic flushing with fresh water is needed to reduce salt accumulation.

Geologically, the land is a recently emerged and youthful terrain. In the southeastern quadrant below surface debris, Eocene limestone (the Damman formation) has been raised in a long, north-oriented dome. In and below this formation lie the vast oil pools. In the western and northern quadrants, layers of continental sand, gravel, silt and sandy clay three hundred or more meters in depth overlie the Damman limestone. The upper part of these beds, the Dibdibba, and possibly also the lower third, the Gar formation, are parts of a mass of sediment deposited by the great wadi whose most recent channel was the Wadi el Batin, which forms the western boundary of the country. There are at least two structural highs in northern Kuwait, and one of them, the Raudhatain uplift, has formed a ground water trap on the western side. Fresh water has been found here, and is continuous throughout an area of about 100 square kilometers. It may have originated during the pluvial periods of the Pleistocene ice age. The supply, though considerable, is not adequate for extensive irrigation, but is being tapped to supplement the distilled water for Kuwait City's municipal needs.

The only other exploited source of ground water is the permeable zone in the top of the Eocene limestone south and west of Kuwait City. The water in it is known to range from about 2,300 parts per million of total salts in the southwestern corner of the country (which might be suitable for irrigation), to more than 100,000 parts per million in the eastern and northern sectors. The source of this water probably lies to the southwest in Saudi Arabia (see the elevations on Map 1). About 6.5 million gallons per day of brackish water are currently produced for non-drinking purposes (a third of a million gallons a day are added to distilled water at Kuwait to make it palatable) or for use in demineralizers. A vast supply remains. If irrigation water were to become available, the lack of nitrogen and phosphorus in the soil would necessitate the extensive use of fertilizers for successful agriculture.

No metallic minerals have been discovered. A considerable amount of limestone is available in the Neutral Zone; this may be combined with clay deposits on Kuwait Bay to produce cement. Investigations have also indicated the presence of some sands which might be exploited for glass-making, although their quality remains to be tested.

Petroleum

The petroleum reserves of Kuwait proper have been estimated at more than 8 billion tons, or enough for about 80 years of production at the present rate, which is approaching 100 million tons a year. Some estimates place Kuwait's oil reserves at more than the known reserves of the entire Western Hemisphere, or about 20 per cent of the world's supply. A considerable part of both on and off-shore areas remain still to be explored.

The oil industry in the State dates from December 23, 1934, when the Kuwait Oil Company (KOC) obtained a concession covering the entire territory of Kuwait proper, the islands and coastal waters (out six miles). About half this area has now been relinquished to the State.[2] Oil was discovered before World War II, but development operations were suspended during the war, and commercial production did not start until 1946. KOC is a British registered company which is owned in equal portions by the British Petroleum Company and the Gulf Oil Company of the United States; it has been the dominant factor in Kuwait's rise to fourth place among the world's oil producers (exceeded by the United States, the Soviet Union and Venezuela). Only Venezuela's crude exports exceed those of Kuwait.

Three other foreign companies operate in the Neutral Zone and the offshore areas. The American Independent Oil Company (Aminoil) was the successful bidder for Kuwait's rights in the Neutral Zone when the Ruler put those rights up for auction in 1948. Aminoil shares the Neutral Zone operation equally with the Getty Oil Company, which obtained the concession for the Saudi Arabian share of these rights. Aminoil pays royalties and taxes to Kuwait and Getty to Saudi Arabia. The Japanese-owned Arabian Oil Company (AOC) obtained a concession in 1958 from both Kuwait and Saudi Arabia to seek and produce oil off the coast of the Neutral Zone.[3] Shipment began on March 25, 1961, and at the end of 1962, a flow of about 210,000 barrels per day had been reached. The Company hopes to reach a volume of 10 million tons a year by 1964. A concession in the

[2] On April 21, 1962, the Kuwait Government opened negotiations with the Kuwait Oil Company for the relinquishment of unexploited areas of the original concession. On May 10, the Company agreed to give up some 386 square miles of its offshore concession area within five years. This represented about 50 per cent of the total concession area. ("Middle East Oil 1962," *Middle Eastern Affairs* [Aug.-Sept. 1963], p. 195.)

[3] An interesting feature of this agreement is that Kuwait is to receive at least 57 per cent of the profit on crude production and on marketing without investing in the enterprise. Kuwait may also obtain additional profits by purchasing up to 10 per cent of the AOC shares at cost after oil is discovered. The agreement requires the Company to construct a refinery in Kuwait or the Neutral Zone when production reaches 150,000 barrels per day.

portion of the Gulf in the area of Kuwait proper was obtained by the Kuwait Shell Petroleum Development Company of the United Kingdom, by an agreement signed on January 15, 1961. Exploration has not yet been successful. Bonus payments likely to total more than £20 million are payable to the State under this agreement and a 20 per cent share in the Kuwait Shell Company may be purchased by the State after oil is discovered.

The great importance of the oil industry to the evolution of the Kuwait economy is discussed below. By 1950, production had reached 17 million metric tons, and was followed by a more than fourfold increase during the next decade. In 1962, over 92 million metric tons were produced (including Kuwait's half interest in the Neutral Zone). 1961's production in Kuwait was 7 per cent of the world output and nearly 30 per cent of the Middle East.

Both the natural and man-made facilities for producing crude oil in Kuwait are of scarcely paralleled efficiency. The cost per barrel of crude oil produced in the huge Burgan field in southern Kuwait was said in 1961 to be only about 6 to 8 cents, as compared with three or

TABLE 1: Oil Production and Revenues [a]

	Production (Million Metric Tons)	Estimated Oil Revenues [b] (Millions of Dollars)
1946	0.8	About 14
1947	2.2	
1948	6.4	
1949	12.4	
1950	17.3	11.2
1951	28.2	16.8
1952	37.6	56.0
1953	43.2	168.0
1954	48.1	194.2
1955	55.3	281.7
1956	55.8	293.7
1957	59.0	307.9
1958	72.4	356.0
1959	72.6	419.4
1960	85.6	445.8
1961	87.5	467.4
1962 [c]	98.7	484.4
1963 [c]	106.0	

[a] Includes Kuwait's half-share of the Neutral Zone.

[b] Prior to 1954, includes KOC payments only.

[c] Fiscal years 1961/62 and 1962/63.

Source: Figures prior to 1957 are estimates based on production data. Figures for 1957–62 are Kuwait government data.

four times that amount elsewhere in the Middle East. Crude production is much less efficient in the Neutral Zone. However, pumping is
necessary and a lower-priced oil is produced.

The People

The lack of economic opportunities ashore before the oil era
stimulated the Kuwaitis to attain proficiency in marine industries, particularly pearling, fishing and boat building, and in sea-borne trade.
The latter, carried on in Kuwait-built dhows, the famous "bhums,"
was mainly with neighboring countries, but also extended to the
Indian sub-continent and to the African coast.

The Kuwaiti people have long possessed a distinctive character of
their own. Their seaward orientation gradually transformed the
tribal tradition of the desert into more urban relationships, though
strong family ties were maintained among the settlers from several
parts of Arabia and Iran. Although surrounded by more powerful
neighbors, Kuwait survived practically unscathed the violent changes
in the Middle East brought about by and between the two world
wars. External pressures must have contributed strongly to the sense
of citizenship among settlers of diverse origin.

Official information is lacking on the population of Kuwait before
the first census taken in 1957. In 1900, the town was reported to
contain 10,000 to 12,000 people, probably not many more than were
residing in the area in the eighteenth century. Ten years later, the
population was estimated at 35,000, and in 1937, at 75,000. Attracted
by the oil boom that got under way in the early 1950s, the population
of Kuwait was swelled by the influx of over 100,000 foreigners. The
composition of the population changed radically. The 1957 census
indicated a population of 206,468, and that of 1961, 321,621, an
annual growth of about 12 per cent. However, this may reflect
in part the incompleteness of the 1957 census. Recent data indicate a
considerably higher figure today, probably in the vicinity of 350,000.[4]
According to present estimates the population in June 1961 was
divided 51.6 per cent Kuwaiti and 48.4 per cent expatriate. This is
a little less Kuwaiti than in 1957 when the proportion was 56.2

[4] Based on a registration of the expatriate labor force in 1963 it appears that
this group now numbers over 122,000. This would indicate a total foreign population of about 185,000, assuming the same age and sex distribution as in 1957. This
compares with 154,000 in 1961.

per cent. In 1957 about 80 per cent of the non-Kuwaiti population was male. This had decreased to 73 per cent in 1961.

The great majority of those coming into Kuwait are from neighboring Arab countries and from Iran, Pakistan and India. According to the 1961 census and a 1963 registration of expatriates in the labor force, the countries of origin of the non-Kuwaiti population and labor force were as follows:

TABLE 2: Non-Kuwaiti Population and Labor Force

Country of Origin	Number of Residents, 1961	In the 1963 Labor Force
Jordan	30,990	24,736
Iraq	27,148	6,588
Iran	17,950	33,533 [a]
United Arab Republic	16,716	3,396
Lebanon	16,241	9,000
Oman	13,857	11,804
India	7,569	6,074
Pakistan	7,205	4,747
Palestine	6,635	— [b]
Saudi Arabia	4,544	978
United Kingdom	2,522	1,076
Other	8,335	20,280 [c]
Total	159,712	122,212 [d]

[a] According to the 1963 registration there were 34,875 illegal entrants in the labor force, of whom 30,542 were Iranian.

[b] Probably counted as Jordanians for purpose of the labor force survey.

[c] Includes 10,131 Syrians.

[d] 103,858 working in the private sector and 18,354 in the public sector.

Kuwait has thus admitted many persons capable of contributing to her economic life. Despite restrictions on foreigners engaging in certain professions and businesses in Kuwait, most of the important positions in the government service below the policy level and in private commerce and industry are held by expatriates from Jordan, Lebanon, India, Egypt and other neighboring countries. A feature of the Kuwaiti portion of the population is that their training in the professions and vocations is not so specialized as the non-Kuwaitis'. Professional and technical occupations, therefore, are predominantly manned by expatriates, as are jobs for unskilled workers. The obvious way to increase the efficiency of the Kuwaitis is to provide education for adults as well as children. This is being attempted, but the difficulties in transforming even an inherently capable people into active participants in a modern economy within a short span of years are considerable.

The point is sometimes made, usually implicitly, that some years from now the present Kuwaitis and their children will be able to provide the necessary labor force themselves without any help from non-Kuwaitis. This might be true in a few fields. Considering that the Kuwaitis only constitute one-third of the present labor force, however, the Kuwaiti population would have to treble in order to provide a labor force of the present size. This would take at least 40 years. In the meantime, the Kuwait economy will have grown and the number of jobs will increase. Those who now lack Kuwait citizenship (or expatriates coming to Kuwait in future), therefore, will probably remain an important feature of the labor force.

The labor force would be more efficient if it were more stable. Most non-Kuwaitis consider their stay in Kuwait a temporary one, and indeed, their assured terms of employment are usually short and unemployment may quickly be followed by deportation (in three months according to present rules). Their prospects for promotion are limited. This all decreases their efficiency. If they were planning to stay in Kuwait permanently, they would bring their families (some may be doing so anyway, judging by the increased ratio of females to males in 1961 as compared with 1957). This in itself would increase their stability and, in addition, would create increased possibilities for expansion of the private sector.

The naturalization laws and procedures are restrictive.[5] Naturalization was originally made possible for non-Kuwaitis after eight years' residence if they were Arab nationals, or fifteen years in other cases, provided they were adults of good conduct, had not been convicted of dishonorable crimes, were in the possession of legal means of livelihood and had a knowledge of Arabic. The citizenship (with certain limitations for the first ten years) could then be granted by decree. However, this law was amended in 1960 in such a manner that the required period of residence before naturalization was made ten years for Arabs and fifteen years for others. The important point was that the time spent in Kuwait prior to the date of the amending

---

[5] Kuwaiti citizenship is recognized for all who resided in Kuwait before 1920 and maintained their residence there up until the promulgation of the Kuwaiti nationality law (Amiri Decree No. 15 of December 5, 1959). Their descendants in the male line also are citizens, as are children born of Kuwaiti mothers if the father is unknown, and foreign women upon marriage to a Kuwaiti. A Kuwaiti woman who marries a foreigner normally would lose her Kuwaiti citizenship.

law did not count toward completing the stipulated period for naturalization. Apart from this general rule, naturalization is possible for the small number of Arab nationals who have resided in the country since 1945. Other foreigners must have been in Kuwait since 1930 to become citizens without a waiting period. Arab nationals who have performed outstanding service for Kuwait may be naturalized on an *ad hoc* basis.[6]

It is clear that reconciliation is needed between these naturalization policies and programs designed to create physical facilities for a considerably larger population than now exists in Kuwait.

The Economy

The phenomenal increase in oil production has caused a drastic change in Kuwait's economy. The first important transformation was, of course, the increase in population attracted first by employment opportunities offered by the oil industry itself, secondly by positions in the greatly expanded government service and thirdly, by employment in the mushrooming construction industry. The money wage-scale, the highest in the Middle East and in the higher ranks of the public service possibly the highest in the world, has been supplemented by the free health, education, and other services of a welfare state.

The opportunities which were offered to foreigners by the oil boom in Kuwait were, of course, available on a still more lavish scale for Kuwaitis themselves. Labor was attracted from pearling, fishing, and boat-building into the oil industry and, as a second stage, into the government service, construction and the manifold service occupations of a high-income economy. Naturally, the traditional labor-intensive industries could not compete. They have receded to a fraction of their former significance or disappeared entirely.

The oil revenues of Kuwait flow in the first instance to the Government in the form of foreign exchange. The portion which the Government elects to invest abroad does not have any immediate effect on Kuwait, although in later years the income from such investment augments the foreign exchange resources of the economy. Over the last ten years a considerable portion (20–25 per cent) has been in-

---

[6] Some (estimated at about 50) have been naturalized in this manner. However, naturalization does not entitle a person to be elected to the National Assembly or to hold positions at the sub-cabinet level or above in the executive branch for which only the native born are qualified.

vested abroad. Most of the remainder of the oil revenues has been converted into local currency through the banking system and spent in the local economy for the current operations of the Government for development projects and for the purchase of land by the Government from the private sector. Other sources of government income are insignificant. The foreign exchange with which the Government purchases its local currency resources is, in turn, used to finance one of the highest levels of retained imports per capita of any country in the world (about $750) and to enable Kuwait to remit private capital abroad on a large scale.

By virtue of the credit policies of the private banking system and, most important, because the foreign exchange counterpart was available for nearly all expenditures of the Government, Kuwait has maintained an open economy both for imports and financial remittances. Inflationary pressures generated through the monetary and fiscal system have scarcely existed. Such price increases as have occurred affected mainly non-importable items such as rents and services. Despite the affluence of Kuwait in foreign exchange and the open economy which this has permitted, if all expenditure by government offices in Kuwait had been used to pay personnel and meet the costs of development projects, it is likely that the impact on certain domestic prices would have been substantial. However, the principal means of channeling the counterpart of the oil revenues into the private economy has been through the Government's purchases of land from the private sector. Since the recipients of the large blocs of these funds are relatively few in number and since many are persons of large financial means with a high propensity to save, the pressures on domestic goods and services have been reduced by large-scale remittances abroad and to a lesser extent by the accumulation of bank deposits at home. The remainder of the funds disbursed for the purchase of lands has gone into construction of large modern buildings, palaces and more modest homes, into some relatively small-scale industrial enterprises and into the importation of expensive consumer goods.

Evolution of Kuwait City

Before 1950, Kuwait City was a comparatively small Arab seaport with sun-baked adobe structures of one story predominating. Unpaved streets, an old-fashioned souk and a primitive port for shallow-draft vessels were its main features. The discovery of oil and the realization that large new sources of revenue were or soon would be available induced a desire for a new kind of community. Town planning, rather than more comprehensive economic development programming, was undertaken. When the construction program was first started about 1949, no one anticipated the amount of effort and time which would be required to convert oil revenues into finished projects. The Government itself was neither organized nor staffed to undertake such a large expansion of public investment. Construction was started largely without plans other than sketches and without even preliminary cost estimates. The first projects were the Tuberculosis Hospital, the Public Security Building and some schools and roads. As revenues increased, pressures grew for a vastly expanded program and this resulted in much more unplanned construction at inflated costs. Street reconstruction, water supply, electricity, education, medical services, ports, roads and housing have been the principal fields of investment.

A city plan was prepared by foreign consultants in October 1951, and amended in February 1954. This is still the basic plan under which the city has expanded from the confines of an old walled town to a wide area completely enveloping the old city. The present ring road communication system with radial roads leading into the heart of the old city established the character of the expansion area (see Map 2). This was really a street plan, born out of expediency, and not the result of planning based on land-use data or population density studies.

In 1951, five large construction companies were engaged under cost-plus contracts to carry out the principal government projects. Decisions were made and work executed in a manner resembling a military operation. This arrangement quickly became unpopular with the Government, owing chiefly to the cost-plus feature of the contracts. Most of these contracts were cancelled before completion. While undoubtedly expensive, it must be conceded that rapid physical changes in the old Arab city were accomplished during this period. The first power and water distillation plants came into being. Many miles of main roads were built; schools, hospitals, mosques and public buildings were begun on a large scale.

The present construction program is a continuation of nearly every phase of the earlier program, but with greater emphasis on development of outlying communities, airports and low-income housing. In the main, a modern city has replaced the old seaport town. Broad thoroughfares and traffic circles dominate the urban area and extend outward into as yet unutilized desert terrain. New commercial buildings, apartment blocks and government offices have been completed or are under construction. However, many miles of urban streets remain to be paved and walking is still hazardous because of lack of sidewalks and inadequate lighting. Considerable progress has been made in the demolition of old buildings, but congested covered shops and the old market still dominate the center of town. Generous compensation is paid to the owners of demolished buildings and expropriated land, in the form of cash or of new premises in the suburbs. The public works program is reviewed in Chapter 7.

CHAPTER **3** *THE GOVERNMENT*

Basic changes have occurred in the central structure of the Government of Kuwait since the Bank Mission of 1961. At that time the ultimate power of government, both legislative and executive, resided with His Highness, the Ruler. He issued decrees (Amiri decrees) which constituted the legislation of the State. He was not only the head of the State but also the head of the ruling family. In the second function his final authority would seem to have been as absolute as in the first, except for the fact that the family had a collective voice in the appointment of a successor; the succession does not follow any rule of descent except that it is confined to the Mubarak branch of the Al Sabah family.

Apart from domestic relationships, which naturally cannot be defined, the family character of the Government found its expression in the fact that the highest advisory and, in matters of less importance, deciding body in the State was the Supreme Council.

The Supreme Council consisted of the presidents of departments belonging to the Mubarak branch of the Al Sabah family.[1] It had ten members. It met regularly once a week. The Ruler could preside over its sessions but often did not do so. In his absence it had no chairman, which underlined the equal status of its members and to a certain extent reflected the character of a family council which it retained. It reached its decisions by a majority vote.

The 1961 Mission observed that the principal weakness in the central government was a lack of unity and coordination. The authority of the Ruler was certainly all-embracing and this would have made for unity, had it not been that as a result of his exalted position and of the very limited capacity of his secretariat, he was rather isolated from the daily business of government and even from the policy-making centers in the agencies. Below his level of authority, the elements of unity and coordination weakened rapidly because of the principle of absolute equality among the members of the Supreme Council. Each was in full charge of one or more separate segments

[1] The highest administrative officials below the president of a department were the director general and deputy director general (now undersecretary and assistant undersecretary). Technical divisions and subdivisions are often placed under officials with special titles such as chief engineer, collector of customs, inspector, financial assistant and the like.

31

of the administration; there was neither a prime minister nor a party-in-power to bring these segments together. The departmentalization which was the result of this situation was intensified further down the hierarchy by the well-known bureaucratic tendency to build little empires under each chief in the absence of coordination from above.

The rapid expansion of government work during recent years had left little time for consolidation and had led to a proliferation of agencies and offices, often charged with entirely new tasks as the need arose or the idea was put forward, mostly even before reasonably competent staff could be found. The number of agencies reporting directly to the central authority had its counterpart in the number of separate divisions under the director general in some departments. This phenomenon was not surprising if one considered the magnitude of the work performed and the number of problems that had to be met on short notice.

But the Mission felt that the Government and its task had grown to such dimensions that a reconsideration of its structure was imperative, and suggested the creation of the position of full-time Chairman of the Supreme Council, an office that would be somewhat analogous to the function of prime minister in other governments. The Chairman would have been given the authority to (1) conduct the meetings of the Council, if acceptable, with a casting vote; (2) be the chief of the Council's Secretariat; and (3) have under his leadership certain institutions of a central importance for coordination and integration. The other presidents were to remain in full charge of their departments, reconstituted and reduced in number. But activities and measures that required general coordination or applied to the entire administration were to be directed, as much as possible, by the Chairman of the Supreme Council. The central government organization proposed by the Mission was as indicated in the accompanying chart of the Central Government Organization proposed by the 1961 Mission.

On November 11, 1962, the Ruler promulgated a written constitution for Kuwait which had been drafted by a constitutent assembly. The Constitution established the Office of Prime Minister, with somewhat the same responsibilities which the 1961 Mission had suggested for the Chairman of the Supreme Council, the latter having now been converted into a Council of Ministers.[2] The other fundamental change effected by the Constitution was the establishment of a Na-

[2] Former presidents are now ministers, and departments are ministries.

CHART I

CHART OF THE PROPOSED CENTRAL GOVERNMENT ORGANIZATION

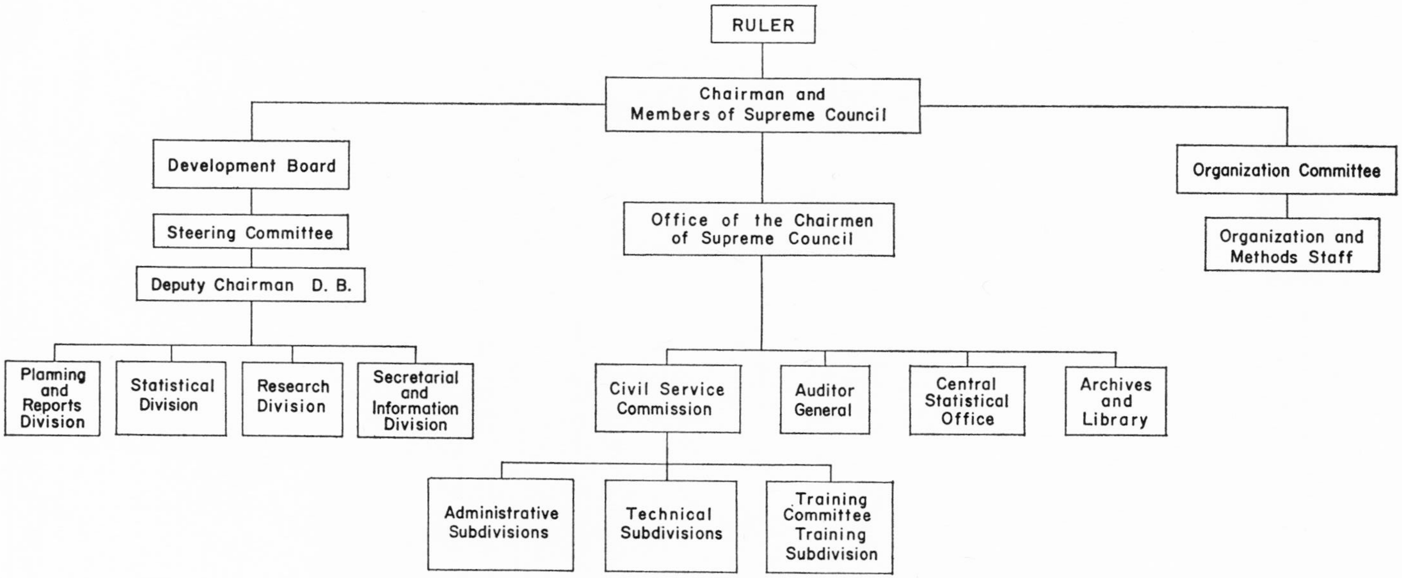

tional Assembly, elected by popular vote and vested with the legislative power. There are 50 elected deputies representing the 10 con-
stituencies into which the State is divided. Ministers who are not
elected members of the National Assembly attend it as *ex-officio*
members. However, at least one minister must be an elected member
of the Assembly. The ministers, appointed by the Ruler as Chief of
State, are severally responsible to the National Assembly for the affairs
of their ministries and are required to resign if given a vote of no
confidence.

The Prime Minister is not subject to no-confidence votes, but if
the Assembly decides that it cannot cooperate with him, the Ruler
may either appoint a new Prime Minister and Cabinet or dissolve
the Assembly and have an election. The Prime Minister may not hold
a ministry portfolio. He presides over the meetings of the Council of
Ministers and the Planning Board. At present the heir designate,
Sheikh Sabah Al Salem Al Sabah, a brother of the Ruler, is the Prime
Minister. Perhaps the most important role of the Prime Minister
at present is to act as liaison between the Ruler and the Assembly.

The 1963 Mission confined its work on public administration to the
features of the new government organization of particular economic
interest such as the Planning Board which is discussed in Chapter 7.
However, since the organization of public functions below the level of
the Ruler and National Assembly prescribed by the Constitution are
now under study, the analysis of the 1961 Mission on this matter
(amended as necessary by subsequent developments) should be of
interest.

There exist, as yet, no organizational decrees covering the structure
of the government in its main aspect, nor is there any agency to study
this matter and to formulate proposals for improvement and better
definition. Jurisdictional conflicts cannot be tested on their merits.
There is no complete "job description" of the departments and
other agencies of the government. In some cases jurisdictional conflicts have developed and have not been solved.

The matter should be studied systematically and proposals should
be drafted to provide a better definition of the jurisdictional limits of
the various agencies and where necessary for the revision of such definitions as exist already. The need for attention to organization exists
both for the general structure of the Government and for the internal
construction of the departments and other agencies. This kind of revision is an endless process in every living administration, but its im-

portance in the present state of Kuwait is such that a central body or committee should be created for the purpose.[3]

Two major functions are envisaged for the committee. These are: (1) to prepare the necessary decrees and regulations that may be required to implement major recommendations on public administration and (2) to function as a consultative body on methods and procedures for improvement of the detailed administrative machinery of the Government. The committee should consist of undersecretaries. It should have a full-time chairman with rank of undersecretary. He should, of course, be a highly respected and senior person experienced in administrative and legal matters. Any outside expert giving assistance on government organization and method problems should be attached to the committee. The committee should report to the Council of Ministers and the Ruler.

The Ministries

There are at present 14 ministries,[4] as compared with the 19 that existed at the time of the 1961 Mission. The functions of six of these (Land Registration, State Domains, Housing, Customs, Port and Orphans) have been taken over by other ministries; one (Civil Service) has been placed directly under the Council of Ministers as the Civil Service Commission; and two new ministries (Commerce and Foreign Affairs) have been established.[5] The reduction is along the lines suggested by the 1961 Mission.

Municipality. In addition to these ministries there is the Kuwait Municipality, which is not a ministry but in some respects functions as such. It is of such an unusual character as to require some discussion. The Municipality is co-extensive with the State of Kuwait. Its Council has a general representative character for the whole country, albeit at a limited level of authority. It consists of a mayor of ministerial rank appointed by decree, and 12 private Kuwaiti

[3] The UN Resident Representative in Kuwait, Mr. S. Kar, has proposed a draft report on government reorganization which he kindly made available to the 1963 Bank Mission. Many of his suggestions on department organization are similar to the conclusions of the 1961 Bank Mission.

[4] Foreign Affairs; Finance and Industry; Commerce; Defense; Public Works; Education; Health; Justice; Post, Telegraph and Telephone; Social Affairs and Labor; Interior; Guidance and Information; Electricity and Water; and Awquaf.

[5] The former Department of Police and Security is now the Ministry of Interior, and Printing and Publishing has evolved into the Ministry of Guidance and Information.

members. The position of the mayor as described in the Kuwait Municipality Ordinance (Amiri Decree 1960 No. 20) is not very clear. As the present mayor is head of both the Public Works Ministry and the Municipality he is a full member of the Council of Ministers. The explanatory note accompanying the Ordinance, however, indicates that as mayor he differs from the members of the Council of Ministers, representing the local government vis-à-vis the Council and the other ministries.

Of the 12 private members of the Municipal Council, eight are to be elected on the basis of a decree that has not yet been issued. The four others are to be appointed by decree on nomination by the mayor from among the "estate owners, merchants, contractors and business owners" of the city. The present Council has 12 appointed members, most of them, if not all, belonging to the enumerated categories and all from Kuwait City. Their selection followed an effort to have them elected by a limited number of prominent citizens. This effort did not succeed, but it did provide a list of candidates from which the appointments were made.

Prior to the adoption of the Constitution, the Municipal Council apparently was intended to be the only elected body representing the entire country. Recently, however, there seems to have been considerable uncertainty about what, if any, is its present role, now that the National Assembly exists. The election of a new Council (mandates of the old one were supposed to expire June 20, 1962) has been repeatedly postponed. The 1963 Mission was told that a new law for the Municipality was being considered as part of the general government reorganization. Many of the functions of the Municipality have been transferred to the Ministry of Public Works and the Planning Board. In a country of larger extent and with a number of cities it would be natural for the present Municipality to concentrate only on the local government of Kuwait City and have other local bodies elsewhere. This is particularly true since its staff, its daily concerns and its services are almost wholly concentrated in Kuwait City. Other agencies like Interior, Education, Health and Social Affairs, as well as the Kuwait Oil Company, are far more active in the villages. The Municipality Ordinance is written for a city. However, there being only one sizable municipality (Fahaheel) outside Kuwait City, the 1961 Mission recommended that the Municipality be transformed into a Department of Interior and Local Government which, for the time being, should be divided into two main parts or sub-departments: Interior proper and the Municipality.

The evolution of local government should afterward determine whether the second part will in future be split into separate local governments for Kuwait City, Fahaheel and the villages, under the guidance and supervision of a division of Local Government in the Department of Interior, or whether the present, all-embracing municipality should be maintained with a more generally representative Council and a suitable internal decentralization to take care of the divergent interests of its various segments.

Ministerial Organization. The 1961 Mission suggested a number of other changes of functions among the various departments. Since some of these changes have already been made and the new Constitution has substantially changed the background against which government organization has to be considered, only a brief resume of those recommendations that still seem relevant is given here. These are:

1) The Departments of Orphans and Land Registration should merge with the Department of Justice.
2) The Department of Customs should become a division of the Department of Finance and Economy (now Ministry of Finance and Industry).
3) A new Department of Communications and Transport should be established, taking over the functions of the Department of Post, Telegraph and Telephone, and of the Port and Civil Aviation Division of the then Department of Police and Public Security.
4) Radio and broadcasting should be taken out of Police and Public Security and placed in a department being responsible for public guidance.

Since many of the changes suggested by the 1961 Mission below the ministry level are still being considered, this report will cover them in more detail. The most important concerned the laws and regulations governing the civil service. These are still relevant.

Civil Service

The concept of a civil service is very new in Kuwait and largely alien to the manner of thinking and mode of life as they existed little more than 12 years ago. The work to be done for the community was as much a family affair as that performed in commerce, shipping, fishing, and the artisan trades; who participated in it and on what conditions was decided as much on a basis of personal relationships in the one case as in the other.

It is therefore easy to understand that the introduction of a modern framework for the public service has met and is meeting enormous difficulties. At the same time the expansion of the State in every phase of modern government activity and even in many that are elsewhere performed by private enterprise—calls for an organizational effort and a wide variety of skills.

Three major features at present characterize the civil service in Kuwait. In the first place, there are many foreign workers in all categories of administrative, professional and technical personnel as well as skilled and unskilled labor. In the second place, a clear divorce between private pursuits and interests and the requirements of public service has not yet been seriously attempted. And thirdly, classification, recruitment, training and supervision are taking shape only slowly and laboriously in a tangle of personal rulings, political pressures, *ad hoc* decisions and emergency measures. A provision in the Constitution which seems to safeguard Kuwaitis against unemployment, together with the financial powers vested in the Assembly, has made it more difficult to maintain civil service standards.

The compulsion to economize, which has elsewhere often stimulated administrative efficiency, is absent. Inequalities and inconsistencies in the conditions under which various groups and individuals are working tend to be smoothed over by additional allowances and special benefits which require rather sophisticated procedures and an impartiality and uniformity in their application for which the administration is as yet hardly prepared.

The first civil service regulations of 1955 were a patchwork of rules, borrowed from models in a number of Arab countries, which brought no prospect of an adequate foundation. They were replaced by the Civil Service Regulations (Amiri Decree 1960 No. 7) issued March 24, 1960, which are now in force and have been followed by a respectable body of executive instructions and further regulations covering a number of special fields. They were patterned mainly on Egyptian models, and constitute by and large a useful framework for personnel administration that should be gradually improved but can be readily maintained in its main features with few—but in themselves very important—changes.

A major defect in the Civil Service Regulations is that they allow sweeping exemptions from the rules as a part of normal procedure, rather than with a time limit. They concern matters of vital importance for the progressive enforcement of the Regulations in their most sensitive aspects. The proposals for exemption emanate from the ministers, who many be influenced by personal reasons or by the difficulties of enforcement. They are submitted to the Council of Ministers, namely to their equals, who may experience similar needs and therefore are inclined to be lenient toward the wishes of their colleagues. The possibility of exemptions should be curtailed in the Regulations themselves.

The most important clause of this kind is found in Article 23, which makes exemption possible from rules that govern recruitment, qualifications, status of civil servants, grading, power of appointment and similar vital matters. A little less dangerous is the exemption from requirements for promotion in Article 54.

A further weakening of the Regulations was introduced in August 1960 (Amiri Decree 1960 No. 38), when a number of retroactive changes were made. The Decree in question dropped or mitigated the requirement of "consent" of the Civil Service Commission for deviation from the rules, and lowered conditions for extraordinary promotions or increments. Though it generally brought improvements in the conditions of service, some of them quite justified, it opened the door for what are probably the most serious defects which the Civil Service still has to overcome.

As a legacy of the past, no clear-cut separation has yet been made between the public duty and the private interest of the civil servant. Many officials in the higher ranks not only are related to merchants' families, which is but natural and unavoidable in a country where that class has been almost the only educated one, but they are also still actively participating in commercial and other private activities. This has its counterpart lower down the scale in the employment of civil servants out of office hours in private jobs such as taxi driving, small trades and the like. This is openly recognized and is considered not at all incompatible with the position of a civil servant. It is an open question whether, notwithstanding the liberal salary scales, sufficient Kuwaitis of standing and ability could have been attracted to the service of the State if that would have meant divesting themselves of all interest in private business.

The operative article in this matter, Article 102 of the Civil Service Regulations, originally said: "An official shall not undertake any other job with pay or gratification even outside the official working hours." This did not apply to the lower category of employees, and seemed not to have been intended as a prohibition against higher ones being actively engaged in business for their own account. An amending article, however, rules that "except with the permission of the president of the department an official shall not undertake any other job . . . ." Of course, a permissive rule of this kind is not uncommon in other administrations where it applies to incidental jobs such as lecturing; the unusual element is the prevalence of such additional work or employment, which often provides the major source of income to the official concerned.

Even though Article 104 states, "An official shall not derive any benefit, directly or indirectly, from any job, contract or tender, connected with the work of the department where he is engaged," the widespread intermingling of private affairs and government work, in a country stricken with the fever of continuous new construction, unavoidably leads to abuse or the suspicion of abuse. As the schools that now offer every child in Kuwait an education begin to increase the number of educated people and widen the strata of society from which officials can be recruited, stricter application of rules against conflict of interest should be enforced.

Number, Qualifications and Training of Civil Servants. It seems clear that there are many unqualified employees in the Kuwait civil service. While educational background is not the only basis of judging the capacity of a person to perform, it is certainly of great importance, particularly in the public service. The 1963 Mission was told that less than 1 per cent of the Kuwaitis in the classified civil service are college graduates, less than 5 per cent have graduated from secondary school and only 13 per cent from primary school. Three thousand, or nearly 30 per cent, were rated as illiterates. These data perhaps are less a gauge of inefficiency than of the redundancy in the government work force.

Accurate statistics on the actual number of government workers, however, or of the breakdown between citizens and expatriates, is not available. For the classified employees, the total appears to be about 36,300, of which 46 per cent (about 16,700) are Kuwaitis and 54 per cent (about 19,600) are expatriates. In addition, there are said to be about 23,000 daily workers, most of whom are employed in construction activities. These data do not cover the military services nor the uniformed police.

The subject of training in the government service certainly requires attention, as does the problem of finding productive employment for the large number who draw pay without performing even a nominal service. Some responsible officials suggest that a minimum of secondary school education be required for the classified workers, and that about 9,000 be relieved of jobs and supported at public expense while they are being educated. This proposal seems to have merit.

It would not be fair to imply that the problem of redundancy in the public service is entirely that of keeping as many Kuwaitis as possible on the public payroll. Kuwait seems to follow a fairly liberal policy of employing expatriates as well, although at present there are strong pressures to reduce their number. It would be calamitous if, at this stage of the education of Kuwaitis, these pressures should prevail, since non-Kuwaiti personnel are particularly needed in those functions which require professional and technical knowledge. Although the top positions, particularly of undersecretary and assistant undersecretary of a department, are reserved for Kuwaitis, the percentage of non-Kuwaitis in the grades just below those two is higher than further down the scale. The vast majority are Arabs, with Iranians, Indians and Pakistanis well behind them. Others are few in number though usually highly qualified. Without these foreign officials and employees, the business of government simply could not be done; and it is a fortunate circumstance that Kuwait has been able to draw on the reservoir that an earlier modern training has created in such countries as the United Arab Republic, Palestine, Jordan, Lebanon and Iraq, where the same language is spoken. A similar situation, it may be noted, obtains in the private sector, from the Kuwait Oil Company down to the smaller shops and trades. At the same time, the surrounding countries provide Kuwait with a large part of the laborers it needs, both unskilled and skilled, and with those who do the domestic and other menial work which is not sought by the Kuwaitis.

The main differences between Kuwaitis and non-Kuwaitis as civil servants are that only the former can obtain permanent appointments, that certain posts, particularly the highest ones, are reserved for them, and that they are entitled to a pension, whereas the non-Kuwaitis receive a gratuity calculated on a lower actuarial basis. In recruitment, Kuwaitis have a preference, require lower qualifications for the same grade, and in practice they are also preferred in promotion. The general disabilities attached to the status of foreigners in Kuwait, of course, also apply to non-Kuwaiti civil servants. The most important drawback in their position, however, is insecurity. The duration of their contracts is for an initial period of two years for officials (with automatic extensions for one year) and of six months or one year for employees (with six months' or one year's extensions). Both, however, are subject to termination with two months' notice. These arrangements make all expatriates liable to termination for which no reason need be given. This does not foster devotion to duty or good morale.

Rapid replacement of the non-Kuwaiti staff by adequately trained Kuwaitis in the higher grades and the more essential functions does not seem possible. Even with a further expansion that may be expected in educational opportunities in Kuwait, and with a lavish program of scholarships abroad, it would probably be optimistic to expect a much larger crop than some 60 academic and some 100 vocational graduates annually in the coming years. These will have to furnish the private as well as the public sector with much-needed personnel. In 1963/64 there were about 545 Kuwaiti students studying abroad on government scholarships. This compares with 521 in 1960/61. The 1963 Mission was informed that the number of students being sent abroad with government scholarships may be reduced as a result of more stringent academic requirements for granting this assistance. The 1961 Mission had suggested a more careful selection of these scholars.

The matter of both pre-entry and in-service training for the public service requires urgent attention and organization. If a suitable set of courses at the lower and lower-middle levels of administration can be designed, participation in these courses might be made compulsory for insufficiently qualified personnel; for some of them, even elementary instruction in writing and mathematics could be added. At the higher-middle level, somewhat more advanced instruction could be organized in general social and economic subjects and in the functioning and aims of various departments, such as has already been attempted by Social Affairs.

The program should be based on a close cooperation with the Ministries of Education, Social Affairs and Finance. More technical instruction should be left to the ministries concerned, but can be promoted by regular consultation. Instructors up to the level of secondary and vocational schooling can be found in or recruited for Kuwait. What is needed is the help of a highly qualified expert on in-service training, particularly in administration and accounts, who should assist in the organization of a new training division in the Civil Service Commission. The expert should be able to speak and write Arabic. An example of this kind of training can be found in Cairo at the Institute of Public Administration.

For an adequate program of scholarships abroad, a more systematic evaluation of the needs of Kuwait and its public services is necessary, as well as a more complete exploration of suitable host countries and institutions for this purpose. Scholarships can then be offered with those needs and educational opportunities fully in mind. Estimates of those needs should be made well before the selection of scholars and in full consultation with all the agencies and, as far as feasible, with the private sector.

Salaries and Wages, Allowances, Retirement Pay. The salary system of Kuwait is simple. It covers in its lowest scale (Group IV) only employees of the messenger variety and includes everybody else, from clerks and typists up to senior graduates in two scales (Groups II and III), divided into four grades each. Group I contains the highest ranking officials only.

Although this system may have too little flexibility in the long run, it does not seem advisable for the moment to propose any important changes. The process of fitting all civil servants into these scales and grades has hardly been completed. A change now would be utterly disturbing, and proposals for revision should wait until more experience has been gained.[6]

Taking into consideration the various allowances and the difference in hours and tempo of work, the salaries and wages compare reasonably well with those paid by major private employers in Kuwait. Apart from salaries and wages civil servants receive a variety of benefits in the form of housing, either rent free or at a low cost, housing and transportation allowances (see Statistical Annex Table XII), allowances for living outside the city, for special skills or hardships, etc.[7] Overtime is paid to the lower categories of civil servants and wage earners.

Of the personnel costs included in the 1960/61 budget of about KD 33 million (excluding the police), about 79 per cent was for salaries and wages and 21 per cent for various allowances. This does not include such benefits as transport, electricity and free social services. The average income of government personnel (again excluding

[6] A difficulty may be caused in the long run by the small number of grades. If the highest grades in each group are destined for selected officials and the posts in those remain relatively few, the point will soon be reached where the annual increments of the lower grades are exhausted and the salary of an official may remain stationary for years. During the period of rapid expansion, promotion must generally have been quick. In the coming years the pressure from below may, however, become quite strong and the danger of inflation of the number of higher positions may increase.

[7] Physicians, dentists, pharmacists, veterinary officers and the uniformed police receive a percentage above the normal salaries.

police), as reflected in the budget is about KD 650 per year (1960/61).

Pensions are liberal.[8] The number of beneficiaries who may continue to draw, for many years, almost the entire amount of the pension upon the death of the pensioner, seems excessive, even though the concept of dependents that have to be cared for is wider in the Arab world than in the Western world. The rules are very complicated, and entail a great deal of calculation and continuous checking.

Recruitment, Promotion, Periodic Reports. The regulations and instructions contain rules for recruitment that are not unsatisfactory in themselves. Vacancies are supposed to be made known, and at least 15 days given for entering applications. Unfortunately, appointments still occur in many cases in a much less formal way, which opens the door for favoritism and deviation from the rules, whether formally sanctioned as an "exemption" or not. Competitive examinations are still practically unknown. The power of appointment is one of the most important personal attributes of high officials. The Civil Service Commission has some control over regular appointments, but is rather powerless with regard to "exemptions."[9] The right to deviate from the rules should be used very sparingly and only in cases where conditions make it necessary or desirable.

The same is true for promotions. Here exemptions would seem entirely unnecessary. From Grade 5 upward in the major groups (II and III) promotion is by seniority except for an increasing part of the available vacancies that may be filled by selection, provided the candidate has served a low minimum period in his grade. Selection is only possible for Kuwaitis. With full application of the rules, promotion can be very rapid for those Kuwaitis who fulfill the qualifications for selection, including two "excellent" reports for the last two years. Group II, Grade 1, the grade just below assistant undersecretary, can be reached by outstanding Kuwaitis in as few as eight years after their first appointment in Grade 4.

Efficiency of Work. Related to the organizational features mentioned above is the comparatively low productivity and the unnecessary com-

[8] The minimum length of service required for establishment of a pension is 15 years, with a pensionable age of 50 years. The normal pension is 2½ per cent of the last-earned salary per year of service. Termination pay for civil servants who have been serving under contracts (non-Kuwaitis) is also liberal, although not equivalent to pensions.

[9] It must be noted that recruitment for Education and Health is rather more strictly organized, particularly for personnel seconded from the United Arab Republic and other personnel recruited abroad.

plexity in certain parts of the administration. These weaknesses are the inevitable result of rapid expansion with inadequately selected and trained personnel, combined with an abundance of funds and a predilection for the most modern forms and equipment.

Even a cursory passage through administrative offices reveals great segmentation, showing little groups of two to five persons performing a few moves in an administrative process. This fragmentation seems unnecessary in what is after all a small State and administration. Supervisors like to measure the importance of their positions by the number of persons and sections they command. There is a profusion of forms and ledgers, often individually well designed and always beautifully printed, which have to be filled out laboriously, in many cases with data that already are easily accessible in other forms and ledgers. At the same time, important data are seldom available. The amount of work done by each person or section is often small because there sometimes simply is not enough work to fill the day. Where office machines have been purchased they are often not used for lack of adaptation to the work and because of shortages of trained operators. There are, of course, many exceptions to this general image, but a classified civil service of about 36,000 members serving a population of about 350,000 speaks for itself.

Budget

The broad disposition of the financial resources of the State is a function which the National Assembly carries out on the basis of recommendations by the Council of Ministers. However, the ministers exercise a large degree of autonomy in financial matters within the limits of the funds apportioned to them. The methods and procedures they follow are based mainly on practices which have grown up separately in the different ministries and only to a very limited extent on regulations or laws applying to the Government as a whole.

Prior to the fiscal year 1960/1961 (when the fiscal period was changed to begin April 1 rather than January 1 as previously), funds were allocated to the departments on an *ad hoc* basis without any formal budgetary procedures. Kuwait's first budget law was enacted on February 9, 1960, and the 1960/61 budget took the general form prescribed in that law. However, as might be expected, the implementation of such an important and far-reaching measure was only partial. Beyond the formal drawing up of the budget, methods and procedures for handling government finances during the fiscal year are still based on old practices, and except in Public Works and one or two other ministries, there are no adequate controls to assure that expenditures are made in accordance with appropriations.

Consideration of the Budget Law of 1960 is an appropriate starting point for an appraisal of fiscal management, and is a good background against which to put the recommendations of the Mission in this important field. The procedures set forth in the Law in general follow established budgetary principles. Revenue estimates, which are made on a gross basis, are the responsibility of the Ministry of Finance and Industry. The task of estimating revenues is relatively easy because of the overwhelming importance of income tax payments from the oil companies, which are based on oil production of the previous year. Since customs duties are uniform (4 per cent) and imports are relatively stable, customs receipts are also not difficult to forecast. The same applies to the return on the foreign investments of the Government. The gross earnings of public utilities and proceeds from the sale of government property may present more difficult problems of estimation, but these items are now of minor importance.

The different ministries are required under the law to submit their expenditure estimates to the Ministry of Finance and Industry at least three months before the new fiscal year begins, and the Constitution requires the budget to be submitted to the Assembly two months thereafter. This is being complied with only in part and one important spending agency, Defense, had failed to submit its estimates for 1961/62 when the 1961 Mission left Kuwait late in April. Failure to comply with the law complicates the job of the financial division of the Ministry of Finance and Industry, which has the main responsibility for preparing the budget, and also means that the Council of Ministers is forced to consider appropriations on a piecemeal basis. This situation does not appear to have improved substantially during the last two years.

The drafters of the Budget Law apparently intended to give priority to the State's foreign investments and its development outlays. To this end, certain percentages of total estimated revenues are supposed to be set aside for foreign investment and development, and the residual allocated for general expenses. Thus far these priorities do not seem to have been observed. Current and development expenditures are considered together, and the amount of the oil revenues invested abroad is, in practice, the principal residual item.

Expenditures are broadly classified between appropriations for construction projects, which are the responsibility of Public Works, and current operating expenses. Appropriations for the purchase of land, the armed forces and the ruling family are each made on a lump sum basis without further breakdown.

Disbursement. Revenues are paid to the Ministry of Finance and Industry. Funds are paid by it, usually on a monthly basis, to the spending departments. Thus collections are centralized and disbursements decentralized. Exceptions are the foreign exchange expenditures of all departments, which are disbursed directly by the Ministry of Finance and Industry, and expenditures for PWD construction projects, which are also disbursed by Finance and Industry. Thus each department has one or more bank accounts of its own on which it draws checks. The Ministries are supposed to report their expenditures to Finance and Industry every month, and on the basis of these reports additional funds are made available so as to raise the bank balances at the disposal of the ministries to certain pre-established levels. There does not seem to be uniformity in this respect, however, and the previous month's expenditures or a fraction of the total year's appropriation, and possibly other bases as well, are also used for this purpose.

The present disbursement system has important weaknesses. There is no real control by Finance and Industry over the use of ministerial bank deposits. Even accurate data for month-end balances are not always available except in the form of informal reports from the banks. In the past, some departments have obtained overdraft facilities from the banks on their own account without the consent or even the knowledge of Finance and Industry. The Mission was informed that this practice no longer prevails.

A more important problem, relating mainly to accounting but also to disbursement, is that the present system, except perhaps in the case of expenditures disbursed by Finance and Industry, does not give any assurance that budget appropriations govern actual expenditures. Apparently it is not at all unusual for Finance to give *ex post facto* approval to ill-defined lump sum disbursements not identified with any particular budget item.

The 1961 Mission recommended that all disbursements should be centralized in the then Department of Finance and Economy. It proposed that government bank accounts should be reduced to not more than one account in each bank, and that all should be "Government of Kuwait" or "Kuwait Treasury" rather than departmental accounts. Checks would be drawn on these accounts by a central disbursing

section in the Department of Finance and Economy against disbursement requests supported with adequate documentation from the
various departments of the Government. The 1963 Mission was
informed that a treasury system would soon be introduced incorporat-
ing these suggestions.

Accounting. Apart from the accounting for gross receipts and for
total expenditures, the accounting now done is decentralized to the
ministerial level. Within each department, the financial assistant or
chief accountant decides on the system he wishes to apply. Thus
wide differences exist, both in method and quality of accounting.
Two examples are indicative of the divergencies that exist.

Within the Ministry of Finance and Industry, accounting is split
up into a large number of ledgers of different kinds maintained by
numerous sections. Most of the accounting is in handwriting. The
bank accounts are booked in several ledgers, one for each bank and
one clerk for each ledger. This could easily be changed into one ledger
for all the bank accounts to be handled by only one clerk. A complete
revision and readjustment of the accounting system as a whole within
the Ministry is urgently needed.

In the Ministry of Public Health, a modern accounting system is
used. The ledgers are mainly kept in handwriting, but in accordance
with a simple and efficient system. Payrolls are made with the help
of machines. The records for each employee are kept on cards in a
very efficient way. Filing is perfect. The stores accounts are kept in a
system of the cardex type. Only a small staff is needed, and the system
seems to work smoothly and efficiently.

Audit. A scheme for establishing a systematic audit for all government transactions is now in the drafting stage. No central auditing
office exists now, nor are independent audits conducted at the ministerial level. In some agencies, however, audits are conducted on behalf
of the officials in charge of the accounting work. The risks of misuse
of funds either through inadvertence or intent are obviously very
great. The 1961 Mission had recommended the establishment of an
office of the Auditor General. The 1963 Mission was informed that
the auditor general's office would be established and attached to the
National Assembly.

The Mission has given considerable thought to whether a pre- or
post-audit system should be adopted. While the former might provide
greater assurance against the misuse of funds or their use for purposes
not included in the budget, we feel that the possible delays involved
outweigh this advantage. The Government should establish a well-

organized audit office supported by adequate authority to conduct
post-audits of all government expenditures and to see that they con-
form to budget appropriations.

Statistics. The 1961 Mission suggested that a central statistical
office be established as part of the central structure under the proposed
Chairman of the Supreme Council. Progress in establishing such an
office is being made under the aegis of the Planning Board. The
importance of improved statistics to the economic development of
Kuwait is very great indeed. A central statistical organization can
never function satisfactorily unless it has the direct cooperation of
those members of the staff of other agencies who can clearly indicate
what statistics they need, for what purpose, and what data their
ministry is able and willing to collect. Only through such close col-
laboration can a central statistical office make it unnecessary for
other agencies to compile their own statistics, in different ways and
with confusing results. Finally, it should be noted that an office of this
kind would be the proper organ to put in charge of the periodic
census.

Delegation of Authority

The present internal organization of the agencies, although
obviously begun according to a fairly uniform pattern, has become
quite diverse. Two organizational difficulties are caused by conditions
typical of the region in general and Kuwait in particular. The first
is the general lack of delegation of authority; it concentrates decisions,
even on minor matters, in the hands of a few persons at the top. In
part this is characteristic of every administration in a state of transition
from the traditional to the modern pattern—when the old structure
weakens and disappears in the flood of new personnel without mutual
ties of family or tribe, and when the conception of entrusting subordinates with authority to act while the general responsibility remains
with the chief is still an unfamiliar one. A civil service in which trust,
ethics and control rest on a common code rather than on personal
relationships grows only slowly.

In the second place, the public puts further obstacles in the way
of the delegation of authority by refusing to accept the decisions of
subordinates and continuing to address itself directly to the chief. This
is a special difficulty in a country like Kuwait, there—in theory at
least—tradition gives everybody the right to walk into the offices of the
highest officials to plead his case in person. This not only slows the

process of delegation, but also hampers top officials in their work and makes difficult concentrated consultation on important subjects during office hours. High officials now are often forced to do the work that requires concentration after the office is closed. A further step in the right direction would be the provision of direct secretarial help to the highest officials, now still very rare, which could relieve them of much work on details and act as a screening device against too great a pressure of visitors.

The situation is further complicated by the conception, understandable in itself, that the power of decision should be reserved for Kuwaiti officials. Since the majority of officials in the higher grades are non-Kuwaitis, this further obstructs delegation of power.

CHAPTER 4 *THE ECONOMY*

National Product and Labor Force

Kuwait is frequently given the accolade as the world's most affluent community. This may well be true if affluence is measured by per capita Gross Domestic Product without reference to the amount saved and transferred abroad or to the pattern of income distribution. Actually, no official national accounts of any kind have been compiled, and the underlying statistics required for an accurate estimate of such accounts do not exist at present.

The Bank Mission that visited Kuwait in 1961, however, made an estimate of GNP for 1959, excluding the retained profits and foreign exchange expenditures of the foreign oil companies. The method, which consisted of extrapolating from balance of payments, fiscal and other known data, is described in Appendix 1. GNP was then estimated at KD 296 million ($828 million) or about $3,200 per head.[1] More recently an industrial consulting firm engaged by the Government arrived at a slightly lower estimate of about KD 285 million ($3,080 per head) for the same year by direct estimates of the various income and investment magnitudes in the economy.[2] The latter estimate also included a calculation that national income was about $2,700 per head. A point of interest, though probably not of great importance in itself, is the conclusion reached in the latter study that, because of the striking increase in population, the per capita income of Kuwait has fallen by 13 per cent from 1958 to 1961, even though total income has risen by 24 per cent over the same period. From somewhat speculative population data it would appear that oil revenues per head fell from about $1,600 in 1959 to less than $1,400 in 1962/63.

Using somewhat the same procedure as in 1961, the 1963 Bank Mission estimated GNP at KD 370 million or $2,960 per head in 1962/63, a decrease in per capita GNP of 7.5 per cent from 1959.

[1] Assuming a 12 per cent per year increase in population from 1957 (census year) to 1959. The per capita figure compares with $2,700–$2,800 for the U.S. for the same period.

[2] Industrial and Process Engineering Consultants (Great Britain). The IPEC estimate was KD 393 million including retained earnings of the foreign oil companies estimated by them at KD 108 million.

The Bank Missions in 1961 and 1963 estimated that about 45 per cent of disposable income is saved.

The findings of the two Missions on the disposition of Kuwait's Gross National Product in 1959 and 1962/63 may be summarized as follows:

TABLE 3   (Million KD)

	1959		1962/63	
Gross National Product [a]	296		370	
Disposition:		%		%
Consumption	163	55	200	54
Capital Outlays in Kuwait	63	21	70	19
Financial Investment Abroad	70	24	100	27

[a] Gross National Product is smaller than Gross Domestic Product by the amount of factor incomes remitted abroad, including the retained income of the oil companies, and larger by the amount of factor income from abroad, consisting mainly of the returns on foreign financial investment.

Unfortunately, no comprehensive occupational analysis of the total population has been made since the 1957 census.[3] However, the 1963 registration of the non-Kuwaiti element in the labor force is available.[4] These data, together with the number of jobs in the 1963/64 government budget, would indicate that the total number of jobs in 1963 was in the neighborhood of 190,000.[5] This compares with about 86,000 in 1957. About 130,000 of these jobs are probably in the private sector and roughly 60,000 in the public sector (including nearly 23,000 workers on a daily wage basis mainly employed in public construction). The labor force is probably considerably smaller than the number of jobs since many people have a government job in the morning and a private job in the afternoon.

The jobs held by non-Kuwaitis in the private sector in 1963 were registered as follows:

[3] The 1961 census data has not yet been processed.

[4] 85 per cent of the skilled workers and 78 per cent of the unskilled were foreigners in 1957. The Kuwaiti participation was most pronounced in fields where neither higher education, technical know-how nor manual skills were necessary, such as in trade, transportation (car drivers), police, etc. The only professional occupation where the Kuwaitis dominated was the clergy.

[5] Assuming that one-quarter of the labor force in the private sector are Kuwaitis.

TABLE 4: Jobs of Non-Kuwaitis

	1963
Professionals	1,292
Business Occupations	14,630
Personal Services	12,904
Skilled Workers	25,640
Transportation Workers	7,342
Unskilled Workers	42,206
Other	744
Total	104,758

Comparable data are not available for 1957.

In addition, in 1963, 19,658 non-Kuwaitis were employed in the classified civil service. Thus it appears that as in 1957, two-thirds of the total jobs in Kuwait were held by non-Kuwaitis and one-third by Kuwaitis. However, the ratio is quite different as far as the classified jobs in the public sector are concerned, with about 16,700 out of 36,300 or 45 per cent of these jobs held by Kuwaitis, whereas expatriates have close to 80 per cent of private sector employment.[6]

In respect of the industrial dispersal of the labor force, Kuwait has a pattern different from nearly all other developing countries. Agriculture and fishing, the extractive industries (including oil) and manufacturing probably provide employment for only 15–20 per cent of the labor force. More than 70 per cent are employed in services.

The Oil Sector

Oil is so pervasive a feature of the Kuwait economy that the different aspects of the industry will crop up frequently in this report. In Chapter 2 the upward surge of petroleum production and revenues accruing to the State was summarized, and the broad effects on the evolution of the community were reviewed. We will treat the retained earnings and foreign exchange expenditures of the foreign oil companies as, by definition, outside the Kuwait economy, and they have not been included in the national accounts data cited above. The fiscal and balance-of-payments aspects of the oil revenues and

[6] Also probably most of the 23,000 day-laborers said to be employed by the Government are non-Kuwaitis.

local expenditures of the oil companies and their prospects for future growth are considered in Chapters 5 and 6. Here we will discuss only the impact of the industry on the labor and commodity markets, and the production of natural gas and of certain refinery products which are produced in or marketed through the Kuwait economy.

The oil industry is second only to the Government as an employer of labor. In 1962, it employed 6,500 to 7,000 persons of whom over 2,000 were administrative, engineering and clerical staff and the remainder so-called payroll employees. From the annual reports of the companies it appears that about 1,350 (20 per cent) of the oil companies' labor force were Kuwaitis, about 2,300 (34 per cent) other Arabs and most of the remainder Indians and Pakistanis. There were, of course, a considerable number of British and American technicians. The payroll of the companies in Kuwait was about KD 7 million. KOC, which employs about 86 per cent of all oil field workers, has been reducing its work force steadily since the period of large-scale construction in the later 1940's and early 1950's. Like the other companies, however, in accordance with Kuwaiti law it gives a preference to Kuwaitis and other Arabs both in employment and providing technical and other training.

The oil companies spent about KD 10 million in the Kuwait economy in 1962 for materials and services of contractors. They endeavor to arrange their local purchases and buy about 85 per cent or more of their total materials locally or through local merchants.

Natural Gas and Refinery Products. Since a substantial amount of natural gas is already used in Kuwait and plans are well advanced for a petrochemical industry that would consume much more, some analysis of the technical aspects of this product is necessary for consideration of the industrial prospects of Kuwait in Chapter 8. Although petroleum in its natural state is a homogeneous liquid, it contains in solution both solid and gaseous hydrocarbons. The gases are held in solution by the pressure they exert on the surrounding strata. In Kuwait, this pressure is sufficient to force the oil up the borehole and along the pipeline to the gathering center. At the gathering center, the pressure is released in three-stage separators. These separators are specially designed so that the gas may be taken off without entraining liquid fractions. For this reason the gas is collected at three pressures: 400 lb/sq.in., 40 lb/sq.in., and atmospheric pressure.

The hydrocarbons which the natural gas contains may be divided into three types:

a) true gases—methane and ethane, which must be chilled before they can be liquefied by pressure;

b) vapors—propane and butane, which may be liquefied by compression alone; and

c) liquids—pentane, hexane and higher paraffins, which are liquids but so volatile that small quantities will always be present in the vapor phase.

As pressure on the crude oil is released, the true gases tend to boil off first, so that the proportion of methane and ethane will be higher in the gas at 400 lb./sq.in. than at 40 lb./sq.in. or at atmospheric pressure. This may be seen from Statistical Annex Table XIX, which gives analyses of typical gases obtained at the three pressures. At present some of the high pressure gas, together with all the low pressure and atmospheric gas, is flared off in the fields.

The quantity of natural gas available depends on the output of crude oil, but at the level of oil production of 1,950,000 [7] barrels per day, gas produced is as follows:

	Cubic feet per Day at 60° F and Atmospheric Pressure
High pressure (400 lb./sq.in.)	445,000,000 ⎫
Low pressure (40 lb./sq.in.)	438,000,000 ⎬ approx.
Atmospheric gas	97,000,000 ⎭
Total	980,000,000

The present and possible future uses of this gas are discussed in Chapter 6.

Refinery Operation. An oil refinery was first erected in 1947 by KOC to supply the Kuwait market and to bunker tankers. The refinery was expanded in 1958 to increase the throughput capacity to 190,000 barrels a day and also to upgrade the gasoline portion to render it suitable for modern automobile engines. Its products and their disposition are as follows:

[7] Average for first nine months of 1963.

TABLE 5

Product	Use	Approximate Quantity with Refinery Through-put of 250,000 Barrels per day of Crude
Propane [a]	Export to Japan	300 tons per day
Butane [a]	Local Market	8 tons per day
Premium Gasoline	Local Market	5,000 barrels per day
Regular Gasoline	Local Market	300 barrels per day
Gasoline Fraction (Kuwait Light Distillate)	Local Market [b]	9,000 barrels per day
"	Export	14,000 barrels per day
"	Reinjected	25,000 barrels per day
Gas Oil	Local Market & Export	60,000 barrels per day
Aviation Kerosene	Local Market & Export	1,000 barrels per day
Kerosene	Local Market	1,000 barrels per day
Marine Diesel Oil	Export and Bunker	3,000 barrels per day
Fuel Oils	Export and Bunker	130,000 barrels per day
Bitumen	Asphalt Plants	100 tons per day

[a] Obtained by compression and liquefaction of atmospheric gas at gathering centers and fractionation at the refinery.

[b] Used to produce gasoline for the home market.

The light gasoline fraction which the Kuwait Oil Company calls Kuwait light distillate, has a limited and fluctuating market. Part is used in gasoline for local consumption and part exported, but on the average, 50 per cent has to be reinjected into the ground. The quantity thus recycled amounts to about 25,000 barrels per day.

General Role of the Government

With an income in convertible foreign exchange close to $1,500 per capita, and a strong tradition of commercial freedom among the important merchant class, one might expect the role of the Government in the economic life of the state to be a fairly passive one. Indeed, this has been the case as regards the usual regulatory functions such as price, wage and exchange controls. Foreign and domestic trade is free, aside from a nominal tariff of 4 per cent. Other taxes are non-existent except a tax on income from non-Kuwaiti participations in domestic business enterprises. In the main it is through participation in, rather than control of, economic activity that the Government's influence is brought to bear on the private sector. However, the dominant size of the oil revenues which are paid to the State, as compared with other sources of income either in the public or the private sectors, naturally gives the Government a powerful influence when it does involve itself in economic affairs.

In addition to producing electricity and water and furnishing postal, telephone and telegraph services, the Government has been a partner with the private sector in the country's most important industrial and commercial enterprises apart, of course, from the foreign oil companies. Private investors and industrialists have sought government participation, both because of the financial resources which the Government could make available and for the preferred position which they assumed that such joint enterprises would have in selling their products to the Government, by far the largest customer in the State. Contrary to experience elsewhere, private entrepreneurs in Kuwait have not hesitated to accord to the Government a controlling interest in enterprises in which they were involved. For example, in the case of the National Industrial Company (NIC), which now owns two plants which were originally wholly in the public sector, private investors have bid eagerly for the stock even when voting control continued to rest with the Government and a majority of the Board of Directors were government appointees.

The supply of loan capital by the Government to private industrial enterprises or jointly owned enterprises is not organized on a very systematic basis. The Ministry of Finance and Industry has made an *ad hoc* loan to the Kuwait Tanker Company, a private concern, at a very low rate of interest, and a relatively large loan was made to the National Asbestos Company. It is hoped that the Credit Bank, which is discussed below, can be developed further as the source of government participation in loan and equity financing of private industrial and commercial ventures. The development of the domestic private industries that exist has been financed by the Kuwaiti owners, either from profits on imports or from the sale of land to the State. In general, loan financing has not played an important role.

The Government has issued a series of decrees which have an important bearing on the economic life of the country, and others, such as a petroleum law, are in preparation. The naturalization legislation has already been discussed. More detailed comments on the budget law, the income tax law, and the decrees establishing the currency and the planning boards are contained in appropriate sections of this report. The Law of Commercial Companies promulgated in 1960 prescribes the various forms of business organizations that may be established in Kuwait and includes rules for their establishment, operation and liquidation. At least 51 per cent of the share or equity participation in the various forms of enterprise must be in the hands of Kuwaitis. Government permission must be obtained for a non-Kuwaiti to participate in the capital of a share company. This special permission is not to be given if the company is engaging in banking or insurance, which are thus barred to foreigners except for existing establishments. Foreigners or foreign business enterprises are not permitted to own outright any form of real property in Kuwait or to engage in business without a Kuwaiti partner, who must have majority control. The foreign-owned businesses established before the passage of the Law of Commercial Companies are required to obtain a Kuwaiti guarantor, presumably to stand good any losses that Kuwaitis may incur from doing business with a foreign establishment.

The Private and Quasi-Private Sector

The conditions under which the private sector operates in Kuwait differ considerably from those in most countries. As we have seen, the amount of oil revenues in relation to the size of the State has made it possible to maintain an open economy. Thus, trade is relatively more attractive than production, and also is more congenial to Kuwait's tradition and aptitudes.

In spite of the freedom of importation, merchants appear to earn high profits. This is partly due to the prosperity of the economy and partly to legal limitations on entry into the importing business. Because the market is small, traders carry as many different lines as possible. Profit rates vary with commodities and from time to time for the same commodity. As long as merchants are willing to deal in almost anything, temporary high profits in a special field lead to increases in supply which bring profits down and induce other merchants to leave the field. This is in the tradition of the Kuwait proclivity for diversified trade. It also reflects the wealth of the merchants and their willingness to carry a large inventory. In retail trade in food, gross profits seem to be high, but this does not necessarily mean that the income of the merchants concerned is correspondingly high. The number of shops, especially in the bazaar, is large, but the turnover in each is low. In addition, the sanitary arrangements are often poor and the waste probably is considerable. During recent years there has been a tendency toward more specialized merchandizing in the newer shops where higher quality goods are sold.

From this background, it is easy to understand why manufacturing industry up to now has played quite a minor role in Kuwait. The first industrial census is now being organized; in the meantime, a satisfactory analysis of the manufacturing industries that do exist is not possible because of the lack of any comprehensive statistical information. However, a rough idea of their scope can be obtained from Table 6, which indicates the industrial establishments registered at the Kuwait Chamber of Commerce in October 1963 compared with those registered in March 1961.

TABLE 6: Industrial Establishments Registered with the Kuwait Chamber of Commerce

Type	Number of Establishments	
	1961	1963
Marble, Tile and Brick-making	34	52
Furniture, Joinery and Carpentry	31	34
Metal and Mechanical Workshops	46	48
Soft Drinks	6	7
Dairy Products, Ice Cream and Ice	7	13
Cold Storage	4	10
Other Establishments	6	38
Total	134	202

These data emphasize the importance of construction materials and home furnishings. Some of the metal workshops, however, are only repair shops for motor cars and other equipment. There are plants producing all the best known soft beverages. Total production is about 100 million bottles per year—satisfying probably the highest per capita consumption in the world.

In addition to the fragmentary nature of this information, some characteristics of the economy of Kuwait make it rather difficult to evaluate these statistics. The number of establishments changes frequently; not only are new workshops established but people readily move from one sort of business to another. This flexibility is probably partly due to a lack of detailed know-how on the part of the owners, who rely almost entirely on hired technical and laboring personnel. Also, many workshops produce goods in a large number of fields; the same establishment may produce tiles and furniture, and repair cars. This may have lead to some double counting in Table 6.

In order to assess the effectiveness of industrial operation, to see the layout, plant and equipment used, and the type of labor, the 1961 Mission visited about 20 workshops and factories. Although they were only a small proportion of the total registered with the Chamber of Commerce, they represented almost all the plants of any size. The rest consisted of men working alone or with one or two assistants. The factories visited varied considerably in size, the biggest employing 300 to 400 workers and the smallest about 10. At least two-thirds of the plants visited were producing building materials. In 1963, the Mission visited an additional six plants which had been installed meanwhile.

In all the factories the wide range of products made was very apparent; thus, products as different as marble tiles and ice cream might be made in the same plant. In addition, the owner was often engaged in some wholesale trade. The small size of the market as well as the desire to hedge if a certain venture was unsuccessful probably accounted for this.

Most of the products were such that high freight costs afforded a natural protection against foreign competition. In the fields where goods came partly from abroad and partly from domestic production, the higher-quality goods normally are imported. One outstanding exception to this was a factory making furniture, where quality was at least equal to that of imported furniture and where costs were stated to be 30 per cent lower than landed cost of competitive products. In general, however, the quality of the products is considerably inferior to that of imported goods. This is due to lack of experience and discrimination on the part of the management. As the efficiency of the different plants varied considerably, profits of the more efficient ones must have been very high for the least efficient to break even. This kind of spread is a typical pattern in an economy where the rate of growth is high and plant capacity scarce. It was encouraging to note that the plants which had been installed between 1961 and 1963 were modern, specialized and technically efficient.

Most of the production of Kuwait industry is sold to the Government, and this provides some protection. Although government contracts are normally placed after international tenders, the specifications and the rapid delivery required give local producers an advantage. For this reason, suppliers of building materials have been mainly domestic.

As we have seen, management in Kuwait appears to have technical rather than managerial qualifications at its disposal. While the first essential is, of course, to know how to make the product, low-cost production nevertheless depends on modern organization methods. Any form of product costing seems to be unknown in Kuwait. After an estimate for pricing purposes had been prepared, comparison of actual costs with estimated costs was normally left to the annual overall accounts to reveal. Thus, no check was possible on profitability of various products, let alone profitability of different deliveries. The lack of specialization renders the problem of effective costing and cost control very difficult.

Workers on both skilled and unskilled manual jobs were non-Kuwaitis. The few Kuwaitis seen were employed as non-technical supervisors, clerks and messengers. Employment of a certain number of Kuwaitis seemed to be prompted by political or public relations considerations. The foreigners were usually in the country without their wives and families, and were housed in rooms provided on the premises; in one or two cases, they were even fed by the employer.

The lower-paid workers usually stay for short periods of up to one year. For more skilled workers, however, employers are prepared to pay higher wages in order to keep a worker in the same job for some years. The normal procedure is for these workers to go to their own countries during the hot season for one or two months and to return in September.

Wages appeared to vary considerably but at a high level. Skilled workers often received KD 2.24 to KD 2.62 a day in 1961, while unskilled workers received about KD 0.75 a day. There appeared to be very few cases where wages were below KD 0.675 a day, the government minimum. By 1963 the minimum had risen to KD 0.825 per day, and unskilled workers earned a little more than this. Wages of skilled workers appeared to have risen only slightly. In some cases where there was a reasonably large production of a single item, a form of piece work payment had been introduced, and workers were then able to earn up to KD 3.75 per day. They probably are able to maintain this pace for only a few weeks at a time and then return to day work.

Where mechanization has been introduced, it has taken the form of machines for individual craftsmen. Very little modern machinery, which aims at reducing the skill required by the operator and increasing output, was seen. In addition there was almost no mechanical handling equipment in any of the factories. All these facts reflect the non-specialized nature of production. With the exception of a few highly mechanized operations, such as a chipboard plant and the asbestos pipe plant installed recently, each factory is, in effect, merely an enlarged version of a small workshop.

Some of the traditional Kuwait occupations still remain. One of these is boat-building. Kuwaiti craftsmen build dhows, launches and other wooden ships. One yard visited employs approximately 30 workers and its capacity is 12 boats per year. It provides one of the few examples of surviving craftsmanship traditional to Kuwait. No drawings are used during construction; the leader decides on the details as the construction proceeds. Only very simple tools are used. For instance, the planks are trimmed to size by an adze, not by a bandsaw. Ten years ago, the shipyard was probably highly competitive, but the increase in wages has not been matched by labor-saving mechanization. Today, the skilled workers are paid up to KD 2.62 per day compared with a rupee a day a decade ago. It is very unlikely that the fishing boats built by the shipyard can compete with modern steel boats.

New Share Companies. Under the Law of Commercial Companies mentioned above, 22 share companies have been established. They are listed in Statistical Annex Table XVIII. The Government participates in the equity of about half these enterprises.

Six of these companies are in banking and insurance, which are discussed in the next chapter. The Kuwait Cinema Company is the only establishment allowed to show films to the Kuwaiti public; it operates seven cinemas. The Kuwait Airlines now entirely owned by the Government, has routes to other Arab countries, India, Iran and Europe.

The Oil Tanker Company owns a tanker (registered tonnage 46,000) which is on charter. The crew are entirely foreign. Two additional tankers of the same size are on order. Besides operating tankers, the Tanker Company distributes liquid gas in Kuwait.

The Kuwait National Petroleum Company (KNPC) took over the local distribution and sale of gasoline from KOC. In addition, it is expected to be the instrument for future Kuwait participation in the extraction of crude oil and the production of oil products. KOC has now relinquished to the Government half of its former concession area, and KNPC is considering the construction of a refinery.

These two companies, together with the Petrochemicals Company discussed later, provide the opportunity for the private sector in Kuwait to participate in various aspects of the oil industry. All of them are planned to command substantial capital, but the contribution of the private sector has so far been limited. Only KD 1.5 million worth of the shares of the Tanker Company have been subscribed and it has largely been financed by a loan of about KD 3 million from the Government. The Government now owns 60 per cent of the shares in the National Petroleum Company. The Petrochemicals Company will start operation with the erection of the fertilizer plant at Shuaibh, an industrial estate being constructed for large-scale industry in southern Kuwait.

In accordance with the Government's policy of giving maximum encouragement to private enterprise in the fields of industry, the regular agencies of the Government no longer manage any industrial installations, apart from an asphalt plant and maintenance workshops belonging to the Public Works Ministry (previously the Public Works Department, or PWD). Until 1960 the Sand-Lime Brick Plant and the Cement Products factories were owned and run by the PWD.

The business community felt that these factories were over-staffed and could be run more efficiently under private management. The Government therefore decided to form a share company with private participation. The company thus formed, the National Industries Company, divided its equity 51 per cent to the Government and 49 per cent to the private sector. The government subscription was paid in kind by turning over to the new Company the brick and cement-products plants. The intention was that the capital raised by public subscription should be used by the Company to extend its operations and finance several subsidiaries.

Before large-scale constructional work in the community started, bricks were imported from Iraq. Heavy freight charges made these very expensive, and an attempt was made to substitute concrete blocks. Apart from the inferior appearance, it was found that exterior walls built of blocks transmitted an inordinate amount of heat. A brick-making plant was therefore built to supply both public and private projects with bricks suitable for exterior walls. The plant also produces small quantities of engineering bricks, hydrated lime and road filler made from finely ground brick dust.

As with all process industries, the level of production has a profound effect on product costs. Labor costs at the plant could be reduced by method study and modern management techniques. If this were done, even working at two-thirds of the rated output, a good profit could be earned. The management structure is far too elaborate and the overhead is excessive. Between 1961 and 1963 the plant was made profitable by raising the selling price of bricks by some 60 per cent. Plans are now in hand, however, to raise the efficiency of the plant and reduce the selling price substantially. The Government will then use bricks for the "limited income" housing schemes.

The cement-products plant was originally erected to produce prefabricated houses, but these were not a success, and production has since concentrated on such cement products as concrete pipe, blocks and tile. The plant is well run, but production could be increased and costs reduced by improved organization of the work. The main reason why costs are above selling price, however, is the low volume of sales. Costs per unit of output for some of its products are as much as 30–40 per cent higher than in 1959, when near capacity production was attained.

Marine Products. Fishing and pearling were important industries in old Kuwait. Both used labor-intensive, old-fashioned methods. Fishing was from dhows without engine power, and pearling was carried on without benefit of aqualungs or other diving gear. Today, with high unit labor costs in Kuwait and stronger international competition, these methods do not suffice. In addition, the international market for pearls has been deteriorating, and better income possibilities are available on land, so pearl diving has ceased. Fishing by traditional methods has been of declining importance too, and today few Kuwaitis are occupied in fishing. Their catches are brought to Kuwait for domestic consumption; but the main part of the local consumption of fish is met by deliveries from foreigners fishing in the Gulf. Some of the latter, however, stay in Kuwait more or less permanently. The fish is auctioned on the local market. Retail prices are often more than twice the auctioned prices. The big gross retail profits are partly offset by inefficient distribution, with high costs caused by waste due to unhygienic conditions.

A modern development in fishing started in 1959, when the Gulf Fisheries Company began operations, with main emphasis on shrimp. Total investment in the Company is about KD 187,000. It is a private Kuwait-owned firm, which in 1961 had a fleet of three trawlers. The total crew of the three boats was from 40 to 50 men, most of them non-Kuwaitis. Catches of fish, other than shrimp, are sold in Kuwait; they do not play an important role in the earnings of the Company. Since 1961, the Company has expanded considerably and is now reported to operate 14 boats.

So far, the attitude of the Government of Kuwait toward large-scale fishing of this type has been influenced by a wish to protect traditional small-scale fishing and to assure ample supplies for the local market. The trawlers are only allowed to fish outside coastal waters (six miles out), the inshore areas being reserved for small-scale fishing. However, shrimp exports have been limited to a large-size shrimp of which the home consumption is low. Apparently, the Government wishes to limit the scope of operations of the large-scale industry to help the small fishermen, but to require that certain of its products be sold only in Kuwait. This policy is not very consistent, since limiting the type of fish that may be exported by the large-scale industry seems likely to increase supplies on the local market and thus reduce the profits from small-scale fishing.

In June 1963, a public company (Kuwait National Fisheries Company) was established with the object of reviving interest of Kuwaitis in fishing. The plan is to build five or six standard trawlers with a supply ship. The trawlers would be kept permanently at sea with relief crews, while the supply ship would have refrigerated storage and a fish meal plant to process the offal. The scheme is being worked out with the help of FAO. It is hoped to obtain Japanese assistance in carrying out a fisheries survey of Gulf waters and to send young men to Japan for training.

Agriculture. Owing to lack of water, agriculture is very restricted and virtually all food is imported. There are signs, however, that an increasing interest is being taken in agriculture. A government experimental farm has been established, primarily to test crops which can be grown with brackish water. This has produced plants and trees which are used in the public gardens and to line the streets. Two decorative trees, prosopus and parkinsonia, are widely used; oleander, stocks, verbena, and petunia flourish. Certain types of eucalyptus trees have been planted as windbreaks.

The government farm has some 20 acres under cultivation and looks after all government gardens—in all about 700 acres. All this area is irrigated with brackish water with a total dissolved solids content of some 4,000 parts per million—of which chlorides are 1,000 parts. It seems inevitable that the salt content of the soil will rise as irrigation continues. This will stunt plant growth and may even kill the plants if some form of leaching with fresh water is not undertaken.

The farm has grown many types of vegetables, and has measured the yield and the irrigation water used. In Statistical Annex Table X the vegetables are listed and arranged in order of preference as far as water usage is concerned. The figures are based on results obtained at the experimental farm. For production on a commercial scale, water used is likely to be higher and yields somewhat lower.

The government farm has also a small dairy herd of Friesian, Jersey, Red Danish and Red Sindhi cows. Experiments are being carried out to produce a breed which gives a good milk yield and is resistant to hot weather. Present indications are that a cross between Jersey and the local Zebu would be most successful. There are about eight commercial dairy herds in Kuwait numbering some 500–600 head. Cows are fed partly on home grown alfalfa, partly on imported alfalfa and partly on imported cake.

The Mission estimated that if water is used to irrigate alfalfa the conversion of this water plus drinking water for the stock to the quality of milk produced is in the ratio of 200:1. Thus the cost of 200 gallons of water must be included in each gallon of milk sold.

The farm also has a poultry section, and experiments are being carried out to find the best crossed breed to give maximum egg production under local conditions. As the poultry is fed on imported meal, the water problem does not arise. The meal could no doubt be cheapened, however, by bulk buying of grain and by mixing it with local products such as fish meal if the proposed fish canning plant is built. There also are several poultry farms owned by private enterprises, but these may not be commercially profitable and their owners are prepared to pay high prices for fresh products.

The Mission also visited a very interesting hydroponics farm run by private enterprise. In this type of agriculture all mineral salts required are added to the irrigation water, the soil being used merely to keep the plant upright.

In the village of Al Jahara, there are some wells containing potable water. It is used for irrigation in the village, and small amounts of vegetables and date palms are grown.

Sheep and goats are traditionally herded by the Bedouins, but with alternative employment for their owners, the number of animals is decreasing rapidly. This, together with rising standards of living and increased population, means that about 1,000 sheep must be imported daily. To meet the requirements of Moslem customs in slaughtering, these animals are brought in alive.

Water and Electric Power

Apart from the Raudhatain wells,[8] practically all the potable water in Kuwait is obtained by distillation from sea water. Combined water

[8] In the course of a search for water for a road construction company in northern Kuwait, three superimposed lenses of fresh water were found in the Dibdibba formation. The lenses lie in a small basin behind the Raudhatain structural high, in the north of Kuwait about 20 kilometers south of the Iraq frontier. The lowest lens contains salty and brackish water below and on the flanks. How much of the water is of fossil origin, from the Pleistocene pluvial periods, and how much is from recent rainfall is not readily apparent. The surface of the land above the lenses is an undrained depression (Map 1) and certainly local recharge has occurred, but the deeper waters probably date, at least in part, from the pluvial periods. The wells are currently yielding from 2 to 3 million gallons per day. A 24″ pipeline has been constructed to Mutla capable of carrying some 7½ million gallons per day, while a 26″ pipeline from Mutla to Kuwait City will have a 10 million gallon capacity.

distilleries and electric power plants are operated by the Ministry of Electricity and Water at the Shuwaikh plant and by KOC at Mina-al-Ahmadi; both plants utilize natural gas. The KOC plant supplies the Company's own installations and Ahmadi town, while the government installation supplies nearly all the remainder of the country.

The present government installation at Shuwaikh has a capacity of 6 million gallons per day of distilled water, and 160 megawatts of electric power. The original distillation plant, commissioned in 1953, is still in use. It consists of ten 100,000 gallon-per-day horizontal tube evaporators using steam from two turbines which, when installed, supplied only enough electricity for the plant. The town supply of power came from diesel generators. This was not an efficient arrangement since water distillation should, if possible, be combined with power production. The original million-gallons-a-day capacity of distilled water was soon doubled with another installation of the same type. In 1957 and 1958, four flash-type four-stage evaporators redoubled the capacity to 4 million gallons per day. These units use steam discharge from generator turbines for distillation, an economical arrangement reducing the cost of distilled water.[9] Subsequently, a 10-stage set of evaporators with total capacity of 2 million gallons per day was installed, and power production was raised to 70 megawatts. In 1961, further generators were installed to give a total power capacity of 160 megawatts. Contracts are being placed for extra distillation capacity of 2,000,000 gallons per day at Shuwaikh; this will probably replace the oldest sets. A new power station is being built at Shuaibah for the industrial estate and this will generate 210 megawatts (more than equal to the present capacity of the State) and produce 3,000,000 gallons of fresh water per day.

Charts II and III show the monthly production of fresh water and power. For water the summer peak load is almost double the winter minimum, although as production has increased, the difference is somewhat reduced. The corresponding generation of power has annual peaks and troughs occurring in approximately the same months as water production. Here again, the units produced during the

---

[9] The original evaporators yield about 2.2 pounds of water for every pound of steam, the four-stage flash evaporators about 3.4 pounds of water per pound of steam, and the 19-stage evaporators about 6 pounds of water per pound of steam. Sea water of 45,300 parts of salts per million is pumped through offshore intakes submerged in Kuwait Bay at a capacity rate of 72 million gallons per day to produce 6 million gallons of distilled water. The 6 million gallons is mixed with 5-7 per cent volume of brackish ground water (about 4,000 parts per million) to produce the potable municipal supply.

hot months are approximately double those during the winter months. Peak loads do not, however, show such a fluctuation, summer peak loads being only about 50 per cent above those in winter. During 1963, production of distilled water has fallen as output from the Raudhatain wells increased.

Realistic cost figures for water are difficult to obtain because:

a) in part of the plant, water and power are produced together and hence an arbitrary split of expenses must be made. This also applies to headquarter expenses and plant management.

b) efficiency of production varies greatly between the original plant and the newest plant; and

c) owing to peak load problems, over-all costs are based on a production which is far less than plant capacity.

The cost of water calculated for 1962/63 was 660 fils ($1.85) per 1,000 imperial gallons. Sweet water is distributed from watering points where it is sold at 600 fils ($1.68) per 1,000 gallons. Charge for haulage by privately owned trucks from the watering point is reported to be about 900 fils (about $2.50) per 1,000 gallons depending on the quantity and distance. Thus, fresh water is a very expensive commodity in Kuwait.

Costs of power generation and distribution were estimated at 7.09 fils per kilowatt hour on the average in 1962/63, of which generation proper accounted for 2.34 fils. Power is charged at 4 fils per unit for industry and 6 fils for domestic use. These rates were established early in 1961. The previous rate was 13 fils for both industrial and domestic use. The Ministry has estimated that at the new prices, electricity production can be self-supporting, provided charges can be collected and other services are paid for.

In addition to the fresh water supply from distillation, 85 wells produce brackish water from the upper 55 meters of the Eocene limestone at As Sulaibiya, 15 kilometers northwest of Kuwait City. Total usable capacity is about 13 million gallons per day of water containing 3,800–4,000 parts per million total dissolved salts. A further 20 wells have been drilled to produce an extra 7 million gallons per day. This is estimated to be the maximum that can be taken from that field.

Figures supplied by the Department for cost of brackish water are 100 fils per 1,000 gallons. No detailed breakdown of costs was available but even this figure appears very high for water which only has

CHART II

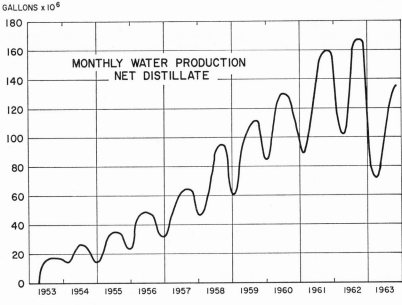

GALLONS x 10^6

MONTHLY WATER PRODUCTION
NET DISTILLATE

SOURCE: Ministry of Power and Water

CHART III

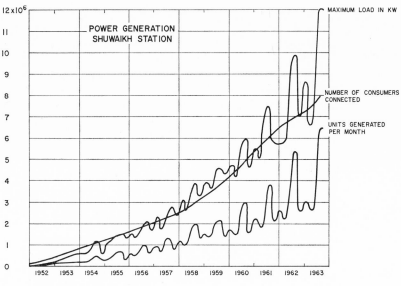

12 x10^6

MAXIMUM LOAD IN KW

POWER GENERATION
SHUWAIKH STATION

NUMBER OF CONSUMERS
CONNECTED

UNITS GENERATED
PER MONTH

SOURCE: Ministry of Power and Water

69

to be pumped and piped. It is distributed free at lorry filling stations with a charge of 100 fils per 1,000 gallons for delivery.

It is planned to install a complete distribution network throughout the city for individual house connections for brackish water. There is a plan for a complementary system for fresh water. However, it was decided to synchronize this scheme with the Shatt-el-Arab project.

Transportation and Communications

There are no railroads in Kuwait and, apart from taxis, there is no public road transport system. There is an excellent road system connecting Kuwait City and Ahmadi and extending north to the Iraqi border (see Map 1). Kuwait also has good air connections with other countries and an excellent seaport.

Air Transport. There is a Kuwaiti-owned airline flying international routes. Kuwait Airways, owned by the Government, has services in operation to principal Middle Eastern points, to Karachi and Bombay, and, three times weekly, to London via Geneva, Frankfurt and Paris. This company began operations in 1954. In 1958, it concluded an operating agreement with BOAC which has now been dissolved.

A private company, Trans-Arabian Airways, began operations in 1959, with services to Cairo, Jerusalem, Beirut, Damascus and Doha. It recently has been bought by the Kuwait Government, and its former services are being operated by Kuwait Airways.

Kuwait Port. This modern port has a deep-water quay, dredged to 33 feet and capable of berthing four ships up to 600 feet in length. Additional berthing facilities are available for two ships up to 550 feet in length and for smaller craft. The design and work on the port is of excellent quality. It was the most impressive project seen in Kuwait from the standpoint of construction and the orderly manner in which it was executed.

Telephone and Telegraph. Before nationalization of the system in 1956, Cable and Wireless Company operated the telephone system in Kuwait. At the time of nationalization the total system did not exceed 2,000 lines and provided service only in the City of Kuwait. The present system is linked with the exchange at Ahmadi, where the Kuwait Oil Company operates a completely independent system. There is considerable room for expansion and improvement in Kuwait's telecommunications facilities, and a ten-year program is under way.

Public Finance

Kuwait enacted its first comprehensive budget law in December 1959, and the 1960/61 and following budgets were prepared, in general, in accordance with this law.[1] The budget is formulated by starting from the revenue estimates for the coming fiscal year. Expenditure allocations are determined by assigning to each category a percentage of total revenue. Thus, if the budget is adhered to, expenditure cannot be larger than revenue. As additions to reserves are included with the expenditures (nominally, but not in practice, as a first charge on revenues), and income on the Government's foreign investment is not included in the revenue estimates, the application of this procedure should result in the constant accumulation of surpluses.

Revenue. In the fiscal year 1962/63, the last period for which complete actual data are available, almost 92 per cent of the State revenues of Kuwait were derived from the petroleum industry and from income on the Government's foreign investments. The Government has no significant tax income from the domestic economy other than a 4 per cent *ad valorem* duty on imports and exports. Even this does not apply to items accounting for nearly a quarter of total imports: chiefly, the imports of the Government and the oil companies, and fresh fruits and vegetables, eggs, cattle and poultry, precious stones and metals. The resale of State-owned land and the receipts of public utilities are the other two internal revenue sources of any significance. Concerning the latter, it is to be noted that the Kuwait budget includes the total gross revenues and total gross expenditures of public utilities, not their net residuals. The only direct tax payable outside the oil sector is the income tax on foreign-owned businesses. This yields very little.

[1] The budget law changed the fiscal year from the calendar year to the 12 months following April 1. The reason for the change was that income tax payments by the oil companies are based on oil production during the previous calendar year; thus, after the end of the calendar year, it is possible to determine fairly accurately the payments of the oil industry during the next fiscal year; royalties, which are based on current production, amount to less than a tenth of total receipts from oil.

Expenditures. Budget and accounting procedures do not permit an accurate breakdown of expenditures, either along functional lines or between current and capital outlays. The latter classification, however, is generally reflected in Table 7.

Current expenditures have been rising quite fast over the past six years; they have long remained around 40 per cent of total expenditures but amounted to 50 per cent in 1962/63, when total expenditures declined because of a fall in the amount spent on land. Defense and security, and health and education, each account for about a quarter of current expenditures. The other most important expenditures were for public utilities. These amounted to about KD 13 million in 1962/63, of which KD 4.3 million were for the Customs and Port Authority.

The private sector of the Kuwait economy is not only highly favored by the absence of any significant taxes and by free education and health services, but it also receives the services of public utilities at low, non-commercial rates. Only in 1962/63 was the total of port dues and customs duties (including duties on goods imported by land and air) higher than the current expenditures of the Customs and Port Administration. Port dues proper cover only a low proportion of operating costs of the Port. The deficit of the telephone and telegraph is also quite large: almost KD 400,000 in 1962/63, when receipts covered only about 70 per cent of current expenditures. The deficit of the electricity and water utilities is even heavier: total revenues of about KD 2.7 million in 1962/63 covered less than half of current expenditures. Before 1961, the cost of the production and distribution services of the Electricity and Water Ministry were just about covered by its operating revenue; however, auxiliary services such as the wiring, gratis, of public and even some private premises, installing street lights, etc., were a substantial burden. The reduction of electricity rates early in 1961, of course, contributed to the deficit. Also, bills are presented and collected on a discriminatory basis, favoring those most able to pay. The deficits of other public utilities are due to similar causes. The situation does not seem to have improved over the recent past. A fairer distribution of the expenses of providing these services and a lower deficit would be very desirable.

In recent years, annual development expenditures have amounted to a little over KD 26 million (about 30 per cent of total expenditures) not including unallocated current expenditures of the Public Works

TABLE 7: State Revenues and Expenditures   (Million KD)

	ACTUAL						Budget Estimates 1963/64	Per cent 1962/63
	1957	1958	(15 mos.)	1960/61	1961/62	1962/63		
Revenues								
Oil Revenue	110.16	127.38	160.29	159.49	166.95	173.00	183.50	85.6
Investment Income	7.11	9.24	9.70	9.52	12.11	14.58[a]	12.00	6.1
Domestic Revenues	5.78	9.32	16.32	14.31	13.71	16.81	12.07	8.3
Total Revenue	123.05	145.94	186.31	183.32	192.77	204.39	208.08	100
Expenditures								
Current Expenditure	38.18	51.41	71.73	56.80	67.46	83.15	99.44	40.4
Defense & Security	8.42	11.36	17.56	16.15	15.41	21.99	22.77	10.1
Health and Education	15.40	20.63	23.44	16.85	17.04	19.52	23.45	9.6
Public Utilities, incld. Customs & Port	7.95	9.07	15.43	10.73	11.50	11.97	13.77	5.9
Other Current Expenditures	7.85	10.35	15.20	13.07	23.51	29.67	39.45	14.8
Development Expenditure	30.75	26.43	38.44	33.48	35.37	35.38	50.35	17.5
Land Purchases	20.47	40.15	84.99	42.93	58.86	46.47	40.00	23.0
Total	90.84	117.99	195.16	133.21	161.69	165.00	189.79	
Budget Surplus	32.21[b]	27.95[b]	−8.85[b]	50.11[b]	31.08[b]	39.39[b]	18.29[b]	19.1[b]
								100

[a] Estimate.
[b] Not including allocations to the "emergency reserve," which amounted to KD 4.9 million in 1962/63.

73

Department (now Ministry of Public Works), which amount to about KD 9 million. Development expenditures show no increasing or decreasing trend. They are discussed further in Chapter 7.

Land purchases are the most important single item in the budget. They rose from KD 12.7 million in 1956 to an annual rate of KD 68 million in the 15 months of the fiscal year 1959/60. After a fall to KD 43 million in the following year, they again rose to almost KD 60 million in 1961/62. The fall to KD 46.5 million in 1962/63 is due to a change in the method of paying for the land acquired by the State. In July 1962, a decision of the Municipal Council supported by the National Assembly, authorized the payment for land purchased by the State of installments extending over a period of up to eight years (depending on the position and price of the land). The Mission was told that the total value of the land acquired by the State during 1963/64 actually amounted to more than KD 60 million.

The introduction of installment buying of land may be a dangerous practice; Kuwait is now in effect piling up public debt in order to finance land purchases, and some authorities concerned do not seem to know the amount of this debt. In coming years, payments will increasingly have to be made for old land purchases; the financial burden of this may in a few years force a drastic curtailment of other expenditures or investments.

Monetary Developments

The Currency. The Currency Law provides that the Kuwaiti dinar may be issued by the Currency Board in exchange for sterling and other convertible currencies; in present practice, the Board issues currency against sterling. The Currency Board Law obligates the Board normally to hold at least 50 per cent of the currency backing in gold and the rest in convertible currencies or financial obligations denominated in such currencies. At present, only gold and British and American government obligations are held. The Kuwaiti authorities are in the process of drafting legislation establishing a Central Bank to replace the Currency Board.

Prior to May 1959, the Indian rupee was the circulating medium in the Gulf Sheikhdoms, including Kuwait. The Kuwait Government obtained rupees by selling sterling to the Reserve Bank of India, and Kuwait banks could convert any excess rupees through the same channel. Because prices of gold were higher in India than on the free gold markets of the world, there was substantial smuggling of gold through Kuwait to India. The export to Kuwait of the rupees obtained in exchange for this gold, and their subsequent conversion into sterling by the Reserve Bank of India was, of course, a drain on the Indian reserve position. Kuwait had a very active free market for foreign exchange based in large part on the demand for funds with which to buy gold. The free rate for sterling, in Zurich and other free foreign exchange markets, had been kept close to the official rate for several years before the return to convertibility in 1958. Moreover, Kuwaitis could readily obtain permission for capital transfers outside the sterling area; and there were no obligations to surrender the proceeds of exports or returns on investment. It was, therefore, fairly easy to obtain foreign exchange with which to buy gold.

In order to suppress the gold trade, the Indian rupee was replaced with a special "Gulf" rupee in May 1959 which, while fully convertible into sterling through the Reserve Bank of India, could not be obtained by selling gold in India. At the time of the 1959 currency changeover the circulation of the Indian rupee in the Sheikhdoms was about Rs 500 million (Rs 330 million in Kuwait). As of March 31, 1961, the circulation of the "Gulf" rupee had reached Rs 540 million.

Of course, Kuwait was not earning returns on the backing corresponding to its growing reserve requirements. In preparing for full independence, Kuwait decided to have a distinctive currency of its own, and to earn the return on the foreign exchange backing previously earned by India. The Kuwait dinar was put into circulation on April 1, 1961; until the end of the exchange period on May 17, 1961, a total of Rs 341.9 million, equivalent to KD 25.6 million was exchanged. The corresponding obligation of India to Kuwait is to be settled in sterling over a period of 11 years, outstanding balances drawing interest at 4.75 per cent. These claims on India are held by the Ministry of Finance and Industry, which, in exchange, transferred liquid foreign assets to the Currency Board. Note and coin issue increased to KD 29.9 million at the end of 1961 and by a further KD 4.5 million (15 per cent) during calendar year 1962. The currency issue subsequently declined, and by September 30, 1963, it stood at KD 31.3 million.

Financial Institutions. The British Bank of the Middle East was the only commercial bank operating in Kuwait until 1952. Its charter still precludes the opening of branches of other foreign banks, as does also Kuwait law. In 1952, a group of Kuwaiti merchants established the

National Bank of Kuwait to do a normal banking business. A second Kuwaiti-owned bank, the Commercial Bank, began its operations on April 1, 1961, and a fourth local bank, the Gulf Bank, began business in May of the same year. No specialized banks or credit institutions were established prior to the chartering of the wholly government-owned Credit Bank in October 1960. This latter institution has very broad functions in the fields of industrial, agricultural, and real estate credit. It is discussed in Chapter 8.

Credit operations of the banks serve primarily to finance foreign trade and, to a much lesser extent, contractors carrying out government projects. While the banks generally follow conservative credit policies, interest rates are lower than in neighboring countries. The prime rate is about 5 per cent, rising for less creditworthy borrowers up to the maximum of 7 per cent fixed by the Commercial Law of January 1961.

There has been competition between banks for obtaining deposits. While current deposits earn no interest, the going rate (by agreement among the banks) on time and savings deposits in the late 1963 was 2.5 per cent up to KD 25,000, 3 per cent between KD 25,000 and KD 250,000, and, subject to negotiations, up to 5.25 per cent and more on deposits above KD 250,000. The time requirement on deposits is waived fairly easily, subject only to loss of interest; in the monetary tables, time deposits were treated as being part of the money supply.

The commercial banks also act as brokers in the sale of new shares of Kuwait public share companies. This is also done by private brokerage firms, some of which publish quotations in daily newspapers. The market for shares is extremely active, and all issues are oversubscribed many times with apparently little regard to their quality.

Only joint stock companies incorporated in Kuwait are allowed to operate insurance businesses. There are at present more than 20 such firms. Three of them are all Kuwaiti-owned: the Kuwait Insurance Company, organized in 1960 with a capital of KD 375,000; Gulf Insurance, organized in 1962, with a capital of KD 800,000; and National Insurance, also launched in 1962, with a capital of KD 1,000,000. They deal in all types of insurance.

Money Supply. Collection of data on bank deposits and currency circulation has recently improved greatly because of the initiative of the Currency Board. Prior to 1963 only year-end data had been estimated (by the International Monetary Fund), on the basis of information provided by the commercial banks and the Currency Board. These data are summarized in the following table.

TABLE 8: Money Supply (Million KD)

	Dec. 31, 1960	Dec. 31, 1961	Dec. 31, 1962	March 31, 1963	June 30, 1963	Sept. 30, 1963	Dec. 30 1963
Currency in Circulation	21.5	26.3	30.6	32.0	29.4	27.8	30.0
Private Bank Deposits	95.5	120.1	145.5	144.8	145.6	148.1	147.6
(of which Time Deposits)			(72.4)	(71.9)	(77.7)	(81.1)	(81.1)
Money Supply	117.0	146.4	176.1	176.8	175.0	175.9	177.6
Increase in Money Supply since Previous Date		29.4	29.7	0.7	−1.8	0.9	1.7

As might be expected in an economy with such large inflows of funds from government expenditures and transfers, bank lending in the past played only a minor role; but this has tended to change somewhat recently. The money supply expanded by about KD 29 million both in 1961 and in 1962. In the earlier year the increase was still entirely accounted for by the accumulation of foreign assets, obtained mainly from the Government as it converted its oil receipts to finance its domestic expenditures. In 1962 bank lending to the private sector accounted for about half of the increase in money supply. The importance of private borrowing from the banks continued to increase. In the first nine months of 1963 the money supply remained stable; a KD 12 million decrease in holdings of foreign assets by the banks (a new development in Kuwait) was offset by an equivalent increase of lending to the private sector and by a decline in government cash holdings. A partial explanation of this development lies perhaps in the fact that the operations of the commercial banks really got under way only in the course of 1962. As the banks took over from the bazaar money lenders the financing of commercial transactions, the need for keeping reserves of money in order to finance such operations decreased. Instead of accumulating more cash to finance its growing transactions, the private sector relied on the banking system to provide for its financial needs, and invested abroad more of its liquid resources.

Table 9 shows the flow of funds through the private sector of the Kuwait economy. Funds are obtained by the private sector through its net transactions with the Government, and subsidiarily, through the local expenditures of the oil companies. They are used to finance

TABLE 9: Sources and Uses of Funds of Private Sector (Million KD)

	1959	1960/61	1961/62	1962/63
Government Expenditures	143.3	135.1	161.7	158.8[a]
— Government Receipts from the Economy	−13.1	−14.4	−13.8	−16.8
Net Government Expenditures	130.2	120.7	147.9	142.0
— Trade Deficit	−85.7	−86.4	−79.8	−93.3
+ Local Expenditures of Oil Companies	9.5	10.0	14.4	16.8
Net Impact of External Factors	−76.2	−76.4	−65.4	−76.5
+ Net Recourse to the Banking System	9.1[b]	1.1[b]	1.0[b]	16.7[c]
— Increase in Money Supply	−29.3[b]	−27.8[b]	−29.5[d]	−23.0[e]
Net Impact of Monetary Factors	−20.2	−26.7	−28.5	− 6.3
Residual = indicated net non-trade remittances (including errors and omissions)	33.8	17.6	54.0	59.2
Indicated net non-trade remittances in Balance of Payments	—	21.2	36.5	76.5
Discrepancy	—	−4.6	17.5	−17.3

[a] Not including allocation to "special reserve."

[b] Figure for calendar year 1961.

[c] Owing to lack of complete fiscal year data the figure for "net recourse to the banking system" is for the 15-month period January 1962–March 1963. As domestic lending by the banks became an important factor only during the course of 1962, it seemed appropriate not to make any adjustment for the extra three months.

[d] Three-quarters of increase in 1961 plus one-quarter of increase in 1962.

[e] Three-quarters of increase in calendar year 1962 plus increase January 1–March 31, 1963.

net imports of goods and services from abroad, and also are the basis for the accumulation of money. The residual is transferred abroad both as remittances by expatriates and as foreign investment by Kuwaitis. In 1962/63, a large portion of the accumulation of money by the private sector was financed by the banks themselves through their lending operations; as a result, more funds were available for private transfer abroad. This trend was strengthened during the first half of the current fiscal year; the money supply stopped growing, and as domestic credit continued to expand, more funds were probably transferred abroad.

Prices. No price statistics are collected officially in Kuwait. The officials of the Kuwait Oil Company have collected some price data in the past, and more recently have compiled cost-of-living indexes applicable to the company's employees. They were good enough to show these to the Bank missions. They tend to confirm what one would expect *a priori,* that the open economy has provided a stabilizer for the price of goods. Little change occurred apart from 1956, when import prices rose under the influence of the Suez crisis. Much of that rise was eliminated subsequently. Other unofficial reports indicate that from 1959 through 1963, food prices have been about stable, except for seasonal fluctuations. This is probably also true of other goods.

Prices that have felt the pressure of demand have been those of land and housing, and of services making use of qualified labor. The price of land in the environs of Kuwait City has increased very rapidly since 1955, mainly under the influence of the Government's land-purchase program.[2] Housing rents, among the highest in the world, have increased both because of the high price of land ("opportunity cost" of holding land rather than selling it to the Government) and because of a very real housing shortage due to the rising standards required by the Kuwaitis themselves and the influx of foreigners. According to an unofficial source, service prices such as those of car-servicing or hair cuts have also risen by fits and starts by almost 40 per cent between 1960 and 1963.

Despite freedom from import restrictions and with tariffs of only 4 per cent, comments are frequently heard that the difference between some prices in Kuwait and abroad is much higher than would be justified by transport costs. Indications are that this is true in some cases because of exclusive dealerships or agencies for some highly desired products. In general, however, the Kuwaiti merchant appears to thrive in a competitive market. The Government, as a principal buyer of many products, can do much to promote healthy competition.

Balance of Payments, Foreign Investments and Foreign Trade

Kuwait has no official balance of payments estimates. Difficulties arise in trying to compile one with the help of banking, fiscal and trade figures, because many figures are completely unavailable, some are collected on the basis of the Kuwait fiscal year, and others are available on a calendar-year basis. The balance of payments summaries presented in Table 10 are therefore only very rough estimates.

The oil companies' tax and royalty payments are, of course, the most important item of foreign receipts. The local expenditures of the oil

[2] In the city, the price of land may be more than KD 8 per square foot.

TABLE 10: Summary of Balance of Payments Estimates   (Million KD)

	Fiscal Year		
	1960/61	1961/62	1962/63
Government Oil Revenue	159	167	173
Local Expenditures of the Oil Companies	10	14	17
Income on Government Foreign Assets	10	12	12
Net Imports	—78	—80	—93
Government Transfers Abroad	—	—	—2
Miscellaneous Private Capital Movements (including errors and omissions)	—21	—36	—77
Net Foreign Assets of Commercial Banks (increase —)	—28	—41	3
Net Official Foreign Assets (increase —)	—51	—36	—33

Source: Complied by Mission from data secured from Ministry of Finance and
Industry, Currency Board and Oil Companies.

companies are composed of wages and salaries paid in dinars, payments to local contractors and payments for goods brought from
local firms or through local importers.[3]

Foreign Investments. Since the inception of large-scale oil revenues,
the Government has followed the prudent policy of placing a considerable portion of these revenues directly in State investments
abroad. The 1961 Mission estimated that about 25 per cent of the
oil revenues earned since 1950 had been so invested. This percentage
was actually a little higher in 1960/61 (25.8 per cent); but it fell to
a rate of about 11 per cent in the following two fiscal years (excluding reinvested earnings on foreign assets and on the assets of the
Currency Board).

The administration of Kuwait's official investments has been mainly
the responsibility of the Kuwait Investment Board in London. This
Board consists of four leading British experts with long experience in
the City of London. It invests such funds as are entrusted to it by the

[3] Oil company personnel might be assumed to spend locally the portion of
the salary paid in dinars, and to remit abroad the portion paid in dollars or
pounds. But all the wages of the so-called "payroll employees" are paid in dinars,
and a substantial part is no doubt remitted abroad. Oil company purchases of goods
and services in Kuwait represent mostly imports channeled through Kuwait, where
only commissions or profits are received on them. Some of these purchases are in
fact paid for in dollars or pounds, and the payments are sometimes remitted
directly to the manufacturer by the oil company, with only a commission being
paid to the Kuwaiti importer. Nevertheless, all these payments should be included
in Kuwait's balance of payments receipts, for the corresponding merchandise
imports are included in Kuwait imports.

State. The policy of the Board has been influenced by the desire
of the Kuwaiti authorities to avoid losses. Official figures on the value
of the Government's foreign investment and on investment income
point to an average yield below 4 per cent.

As of December 31, 1962, the last date for which the precise figure
is known, the Government's foreign assets amounted to KD 374 million
—more than $1 billion. KD 34 million of this represented the reserves
of the Currency Board. Of the rest, about 55 per cent were in government bonds and treasury bills, mostly in the United Kingdom, and
about 17 per cent in shares and bonds of private companies, about half
in sterling, half in dollars and other currencies. About 15 per cent
were on deposit in banks. The rest are (*a*) claims on India resulting
from the withdrawal of rupees from circulation, (*b*) subscription to
international organizations and (*c*) the paid-up capital of the Kuwait
Fund for Arab Economic Development (KFAED) .

The composition of government reserves was substantially affected
by a few large, interest-free loans made recently to Algeria (KD 6
million disbursed by October 30, 1963), Iraq (KD 30 million) and
the United Arab Republic (KD 3 million) , and subscriptions to the
capital of KFAED. Table 11 shows the estimated position of the
reserves.

Trade. Practically all the goods needed for the daily life of Kuwait
are imported. The lack of natural resources (apart from oil), the
relatively small size of the market, the existence of a business community experienced in and oriented toward foreign trade, the lack of
import restrictions, low import duties, and, of course, the unprecedented

TABLE 11: Foreign Assets of the Government and Commercial Banks

(Million KD)

	Revenue-yielding Investment [a]	Currency Board	KFAED	International Organizations	Interest-free Loans	Sub-total	Commercial Banks
Mar. 31, 1961	227	—	—	—	—	227	109
Mar. 31, 1962	340	32	—	—	—	372	140
Mar. 31, 1963	353	35	15	5	—	408	139
Nov. 30, 1963 [b]	320	32	27	5	39	423	140

[a] Includes Indian currency debt, yielding 4.75 per cent and various small loans
yielding 4 per cent.
[b] Rough estimate.

growth of the oil income accruing to the Government and its expenditures in the private sector—all contributed to the rapid rise of Kuwait's imports, and to the attainment of the highest level of per capita imports in the world. Imports rose from about KD 30 million in 1954 to KD 102 million in 1963—about $800 per capita of the resident population. In 1961, the last year for which these figures are available, consumer goods imports amounted to more than 60 per cent of the total, durable consumer goods alone accounting for almost 30 per cent. About 40 per cent of the remaining imports, including unclassified, consisted of building materials and tools. In 1962, building materials accounted for 60 per cent of the total tonnage of imports —roughly the same proportion as in 1960, but 13 per cent more than in 1961.

Four countries provide 60 per cent of Kuwait's imports: the United States, the most important source for the first time in 1962, and the United Kingdom each provide about 20 per cent; Germany and Japan each provide about 8.6 per cent of total imports. The rest comes mostly from various countries of Western Europe and the Middle East (including India).

TABLE 12: Summary of Foreign Trade, 1954–1962   (Million KD)

	Imports	Exports [a]	Net Imports
1954	30.0	2.0	28.0
1955	33.7	2.0	31.7
1956	41.2	3.0	38.2
1957	60.0	4.0	56.0
1958	75.0	5.5	69.5
1959	92.7	7.0	85.7
1960	86.4	8.3	78.1
1961	89.0	9.2	79.8
1962	101.9	8.1	93.8

[a] Excluding oil and oil products.

Most of Kuwait's exports (excluding oil) consist of finished products previously imported. The only non-oil related domestic product exported is fish, mainly shrimp.

The State is increasingly important as a center of trans-shipment to Iran, Saudi Arabia, the Gulf Sheikhdoms, and Iraq. This is due to Kuwait's good location at the head of the Gulf, to its excellent harbor and low port dues and to the presence of an enterprising merchant community. No less important is the fact that import duty in Kuwait is only 4 per cent,[4] much lower than in many of the neighboring countries. Kuwait is an excellent trans-shipment point from steamers to other means of transportation better adapted to escaping the thorough attention of customs authorities. According to one authoritative source, the declared export figures could be as much as 40 per cent lower than the actual value of exports.

[4] Imports of alcoholic beverages are subject to license and bear a duty of 100 per cent, as do also imports of bottled gas. This latter is perhaps Kuwait's only protective tariff. No import duty applies to a number of other imports. There is also a 4 per cent duty on exports, but goods for which the import duty has been paid are exempted from it.

CHAPTER 6 *FINANCIAL PROSPECTS—AVAILABILITY AND ALLOCATION OF FINANCIAL RESOURCES*

State Revenue

The oil revenues of Kuwait are very likely to increase substantially above the nearly $485 million obtained in 1962/63. About $510 million are expected in 1963/64. The general optimistic outlook for the longer run is based chiefly on the efficiency and low cost of oil production and the exploration and development activity now being pursued in the offshore concessions. There also is a possibility of Kuwait, along with other producing countries, getting a larger share of profits from crude production.

Over the last four years Kuwait has enjoyed an annual average increase in oil revenues (excluding lump sum bonuses, etc.) and in crude production of about 8 per cent. However, the year-to-year variations in the growth of both revenues and output were very substantial, ranging from virtually zero to more than 17 per cent. Insofar as volume is concerned, the Mission expects a sizable increase during the next few years as the new concessions come into full production, and then possibly some leveling off.[1] An average increase in volume of at least 7 per cent a year through 1965 seems conservative. This is the percentage increase commonly predicted for the Middle East generally, although the 1962 expansion was over 9 per cent.

The Mission cannot, of course, venture a prediction regarding the future price of crude in the Gulf area. At present, the posted price ex Mina-Al-Ahmadi (KOC) is only 4¢ per barrel above the 1951 level which was the lowest in the last decade. Even if this price should not hold under competition in European markets from North Africa and possible Soviet bloc sources,[2] the Mission believes that increased volume and the possibility of a larger share of the profits will more than

---

[1] Kuwait's new concessions are unlikely to yield as high profits per ton as KOC's production. However bonus, rental and other payments should average about $12 million a year until substantial production from the new concessions is attained. This would be about 2.8 per cent of oil revenues (excluding lump-sum payments) received in 1960.

[2] See Statistical Annex Table VI for destination of Kuwait's main (KOC) crude exports: 64 per cent go to Europe, 21 per cent to Asia, mainly Japan, and most of the rest to the Western Hemisphere. If Arabian Oil were included the Asian share would be larger.

compensate for possible adverse price developments. The new source of revenue from the exploitation of gas, the profits of which are shared as those from oil, also affects longer-run prospects. Therefore, the Mission considers that Kuwait's income from oil and related products may reach over $560 million by 1965. This would mean a relatively modest increase of about 5 per cent per annum from 1962 to 1965.

In respect of other income from external sources, the Mission recommends that Kuwait invest abroad about 20 per cent of its State income in addition to the subscription it has already made to the capital of the Kuwait Fund for Arab Economic Development. Investment income might increase from about KD 12 million in 1961 to KD 13.7 million by 1965/66. If Kuwait makes additional large long-term interest-free loans (such as the KD 30 million loan to Iraq), the decline in revenue-yielding investment is bound to show up in some temporary decline in investment income. A much more important determinant of investment income in the future, however, will be the size of future budget surpluses.

Other State revenues have increased by more than 10 per cent in most past years. This reflects primarily the flow of dutiable imports. The Mission hopes that the public utilities and port can earn larger gross incomes and get closer to self-sufficiency. Income from land sales should also continue to rise somewhat from its present low level.

Based on conservative estimates the Mission expects the disposable public income of the State to follow the pattern set out in the following table.

TABLE 13: Estimated State Revenues   (Million KD)

	Actual			Estimated		
	1960/61	1961/62	1962/63	1963/64	1964/65	1965/66
External Sources						
Oil Revenues [a]	159.5	166.9	173.0	180.0	190.0	200.0
Investment Income	9.5	12.1	14.6	12.0	12.8	13.8
Sub-total	169.0	179.1	187.6	192.0	202.8	213.8
Internal Sources	14.3	13.7	16.8	17.0	17.0	17.0
Total State Revenue	183.3	192.8	204.4	209.0	219.8	230.8

[a] Including lump-sum and rental payments under present concession agreements.

Non-Development Expenditures

In past years, from 35 to 40 per cent of available revenues were used for expenditures, mainly of a current or operational nature (see Table 7 in Chapter 5). These expenditures may be expected to increase somewhat as the maintenance of roads and other public works requires larger outlays; defense outlays also may be somewhat higher. The Mission was much impressed, however, with the fact that probably about one-third of the labor force in Kuwait is on the public payroll and that in the last three budgets, excluding the Armed Forces, development projects and land purchases, over 60 per cent of public expenditures were for personnel. Redundant employees are much in evidence. As other job opportunities become available, this situation should be improved. For planning purposes, an allocation of 40 per cent of total revenues for current expenditures would seem ample. This would be about KD 260 million for the three years 1963/64 through 1965/66.

Disposition of Public Savings

About 60 per cent of the Government's income (KD 400 million) would be available for investment at home in the public and private sectors, for transfer payments to the private sector (purchase of land), or for the foreign investments of the State.

With available public and private savings much in excess of prudent or profitable domestic investment opportunities a first question is the proportion of public savings to be invested at home and abroad. In deciding on its answer to this question, the Mission felt that the following factors were of principal importance: (1) How much domestic investment over the coming years is likely to be needed to carry out useful public projects now envisaged or that seem to be required to complete the transformation of Kuwait into a modern, attractive community and to develop any latent natural resources? (2) How much can the State usefully and profitably invest in the private sector? (3) In view of the special role of public expenditures in the economic stability of Kuwait, what level of total government disbursements within the economy is likely to be needed to avoid undesirable contraction of economic activity and to provide for reasonable long-term growth of the private sector? (4) What resources should be devoted to helping other countries, either through the Kuwait Fund for Arab Economic Development or through government-to-government loans?

As already noted, the new Kuwait Planning Board is beginning work on a comprehensive investment program to start in two or three years. Therefore, the Mission thought it advisable to project an expenditure pattern only for three years or through 1965/66.

In Chapter 7, Table 15, it is indicated that projects in the present public works program are estimated to cost about KD 90 million. However, this does not include provision for additional power and water and for telecommunications, all of which should have a high priority in view of Kuwait's plan for new industries and the desirability of obtaining water for some irrigation. In view of the uncertainty of the Shatt water project, it is difficult to make any estimate of over-all capital expenditures for power and water even for the next three years. In 1963/64, the capital expenditures of the Ministry of Electricity and Water are estimated at KD 10.7 million; it seems probable that about this amount will actually be spent in that year and higher amounts will be spent during the next two years. An estimate of KD 35 million for new power and water projects during the three-year period seems reasonable. Capital expenditures for the new telephone system are estimated at KD 3.7 million in 1964/65. When allowing for some lag in the program, KD 5 million seems reasonable for 1964/65 and 1965/66. Therefore, all told, capital expenditures in the public sector of KD 130 million for these three years seem possible. However, based on past experience, some shortfall in expenditures as compared with expectations may be anticipated. Therefore, KD 120 million, or KD 40 million a year, would seem like a fair estimate of the amount that can usefully be spent on public sector projects of an infrastructure type from 1963/64 through 1965/66.

What the Government can usefully invest in the quasi-private and private sectors is more difficult to estimate. The 1961 Bank Mission placed a figure of KD 64 million on this over the five-year period 1961/62-1965.66; but neither the major projects in petrochemicals and metals reduction, or smaller industrial projects that might have required government loans, really got under way during the first two years of this period. Now, however, the Government, in partnership with Gulf and British Petroleum, is going ahead with a large ammonia-fertilizer complex, and a law for the encouragement of private industrial ventures is under active consideration. A large industrial estate project is already under construction. Therefore, it seems likely that as much as KD 50 million may be spent on investment in these sectors during this and the following two years.[3] This makes no provision for the proposed new oil refinery which is being seriously studied.

Thus total current and capital outlays by the Government would be about KD 430 million (KD 143 million a year), leaving KD 230 million (KD 77 million a year) for the purchase of land and foreign investment by the Government.

Land Purchases by the Government. No long-range policy has been adopted to govern the allocation of funds between the purchase of land in Kuwait and foreign investment. In 1959 the amount spent on land was roughly double the increment to public foreign investments. The final 1960/61 data show a larger relative increment to investments abroad; but in 1961/62 the ratio was about 5 to 3 in favor of land purchases, and it fell only slightly, to about 7 to 5, in 1962/63. During the six and a quarter years ending March 31, 1963, over KD 295 million was spent by the Government to acquire land, or more than a third of total government income. Over the same period, the increase in public foreign investments was about KD 140 million, or 16 per cent of government revenue.

Land has been acquired by the Government in the highly urbanized Kuwait City, in its environs, and to a small extent in other population centers. Lands purchased near Kuwait City are mostly unimproved except for a high-quality road network in the area. The land purchased in the old city has in part been used for roads and other public facilities and in part resold to the private sector. The Mission was informed that such purchases will have to continue at the rate of about KD 20 million per year for the contemplated construction and urban development programs. Land acquired in the area surrounding the City has, in small part, been used to construct housing which has been sold or rented to private persons, largely government employees.

From the financial standpoint, in addition to the fact that over

---

[3] Based on the estimates in Chapter 8 and assuming three years for construction of the industrial estate and five years for the petrochemical complex (with 60 per cent government participation), this may be broken down as follows:

(Million KD)

	Total Requirement	Requirement through 1965/66
Industries to Use Natural Gas	60	30
Industrial Estate	20	15
Credit to Small Industries	10	5
Total	90	50

50 per cent more has been spent on land in the last six years than on public capital projects, a striking fact is the relatively small amount which the Government has obtained from the resale of land or from rentals on government-owned property. Despite the fact that the housing program would seem to provide for the turnover of a good deal of this land, only KD 15.4 million or about 5 per cent of the cost of land acquired by the Government has been recovered by sale in the last six years.

The private sector has probably relied on land purchases for investment capital. However, it is to be noted that to the extent that funds received from the sale of land are remitted for investment abroad, they do not affect prosperity in Kuwait. The Mission has no accurate data on the disposal, within the private sector, of these funds, or on whether domestic or foreign private investment would suffer more from their reduction. However, we have the impression that if the amount being spent on land were cut from the budget without an alternative flow of public investment being provided, the operations of the economy at its present level would not be sustained. At the same time, we are convinced that the purchase of land at high prices in excess of development needs is not a good use of government funds from the standpoint of a desirable distribution of the oil revenues within Kuwait, or as a means of promoting the orderly development of the private sector of the economy.

The Mission recognizes that there are uncertainties regarding long-run prospects of total demand in the economy. It is often argued that the level of government construction is bound to decrease, and that this will not only lead to trouble for the construction industries, but will reduce the general income level as well, construction being one of the most important industries in Kuwait.

Although the Mission recognizes the importance of government expenditures in Kuwait, it does not feel that the growth of the economy needs or should be made to depend upon a rising tide of public disbursements for the acquisition at highly subsidized prices of unnecessary land or of land needed for development at the present highly subsidized prices.[4] There are fairly good prospects for a sizable lift in the level of industrial investment, particularly in petrochemicals. In addition, practically all capital expenditures give rise to future current expenditures: schools and hospitals require teachers and doctors, buildings and roads require maintenance. These will

[4] One striking example cited to the Mission was that space required to park a car in the center of the city would cost about KD 7,000.

channel increasing amounts of government funds into the economy. The Mission therefore feels that concern about the future of total demand may not be justified.

The Mission also has some doubts whether the present prosperity, based as it is so largely on the construction industry, can really be sustained by continuing the outpouring of public funds for land. Kuwait's demands for new construction are not insatiable, and it is to this industry that most land purchase funds reinvested in Kuwait appear to go. If more and more funds are paid to landowners which they cannot invest securely in Kuwait real estate, they are apt to look for the same type of investment abroad rather than, say, industrial investment at home. The Mission therefore would expect private remittances rather than the Kuwait economy to benefit more and more from an indefinite continuation of land purchasing.

These considerations lead to the conclusion that expenditures for land purchases should not exceed KD 30 million in 1963/64 or in 1964/65. This should provide for some repayment of the installment debt contracted since June 1962. Acquisition of new land should therefore be reduced to about KD 20 million per annum in 1965/66 (as compared to KD 60 million in 1962/63), and total expenditures on land should also fall to about this level. Expenditures of not more than KD 80 million for the purchase of land during the three-year period 1963/64 through 1965/66 would leave KD 150 million for public foreign investment over the period, or around 23 per cent of total State revenues. In 1960/61, about 26 per cent was so invested, but the figure dropped to 15 per cent in the following two years taken together.

Summary of Revenue Allocations. The suggested disposition of State revenues is as follows:

TABLE 14   (Million KD)

	1963/64–1965/66
Total Revenues	660
(1) Current Expenditures	260
Public Savings	400
Use:	
Public Investment Projects	120
Public Investment in:	
Private and Quasi-Private Projects	50
Purchase of Land	80
(2) Domestic Investment and Transfers	250
Total Domestic Disposition of Public Revenues [(1) + (2)]	510
(3) Foreign Investment	150
Total	660

This program would permit KD 170 million a year of State disbursements in the private sector. The amount would be a little higher than in 1962/63 but somewhat lower than projected in 1963/64. With a larger portion going for actual investment in the Kuwait economy and a smaller portion for land, the effect on GNP should be favorable.

The other major class of expenditures, those of the oil companies, can be expected to remain fairly stable in the future; the operations of most oil companies have reached a stage where, even if production continues to expand, the related expenditures can level off. As for the proportion of purchases they channel through Kuwait, it is already about 80 per cent and cannot very well increase much further. But it may be that as the Kuwait economy expands, a higher proportion of such payments will be retained within Kuwait.

Foreign Public Investment. Kuwait is not, as in the past, channeling almost all its public foreign investment funds to revenue-yielding uses abroad. The 1961 Bank Mission observed that: "The beginning which the Government has made in investing some of its funds in the Middle East is highly commendable because of the need of that area for medium- and long-term capital. The portion of the surplus revenues of the Government which are invested in the Middle East or elsewhere in order to assist in carrying out projects for development purposes should be made available on terms consistent with the return expected on the project that is being financed. In view of the circumstances of some countries in which Kuwait may desire to invest, some of these loans may be made at lower rates of interest and for longer terms than would apply to conventional loans. Whether the undertaking is a revenue-producing project, and the effect of the project on the foreign exchange earnings of the borrowing country, should, of course, be taken into account."

A very important and gratifying step along these lines was taken when the Kuwait Fund for Arab Economic Development was established at the end of 1961. KFAED was started with authorized capital of KD 50 million which subsequently was increased to KD 100 million; KD 27 million has already been paid in. It makes loans to Arab countries for specific development projects. The interest rate and terms of repayment of these loans depend on the nature of the project. Until now, they have varied from 3 to 4 per cent with repayment over 10 to 20 years. Loans have been made to the Sudan for railways, to Jordan for the Yarmuk project, phosphates and for small industries, and to Tunisia for an agricultural project and a power plant. Commitments for these loans amount to KD 20.4 million. In addition, loans to Algeria and Yemen were under consideration in 1963. Subsequently, a loan of KD 35 million was made to the United Arab Republic, in large part for improvements to the Suez Canal.

Provided it keeps its independence from political influences and continues to scrutinize carefully the economic priority of projects presented to it, KFAED should make a significant contribution to the development of Arab countries perhaps even in excess of its own financial resources. In view of the rising level of disbursements and of the need for KFAED to constitute reserves by investing in revenue-yielding securities, the unpaid portion of its capital should be paid in as soon as possible.

The Government also has made several interest-free direct loans to Arab countries: a KD 10 million loan to Algeria, of which KD 6 million had been disbursed by the end of October 1963; KD 30 million to Iraq, entirely disbursed; and KD 3 million to the United Arab Republic, to help it finance its share of the cost of saving the Abu Simbel Temple from inundation due to the High Aswan Dam. Other such loans may well be made in the coming years, but this is a matter on which the Mission can formulate no estimates or comments.

In respect of the Government's management of its other investment funds, the 1961 Bank Mission recommended the establishment of a high level board or committee to advise on the general policies under which specific investments could be made. A group of distinguished persons of very wide financial experience has now been appointed for this purpose. The 1961 Mission also suggested that there was a need for an institution in Kuwait which would attract private capital, either through the sale of equity or by loan participations, for investments both in Kuwait and abroad, preferably in developing countries. In 1961, the Kuwait Investment Company, with KD 15 million of capital (half government and half private) was established. Up to now most of its investments have been loans, but we understand it is considering some direct participations as well.

Private Savings. Our national accounts estimates (Appendix 1) indicate that private savings in Kuwait may amount to about KD 100 million a year. In 1962/63, perhaps roughly a third of this was invested in physical assets in Kuwait and two-thirds were remitted abroad. Of course, most of this investment in Kuwait was in building construction, but an increasing portion is going into small industries and other more productive assets. With an annual accrual of financial resources of this magnitude there is obviously abundant capital for ventures that have a reasonable chance of success.

Balance of Payments Prospects

Balance of payments problems can hardly be a deterrent to invest-ment in Kuwait. We have already estimated the combined oil and foreign investment income of the Government at over KD 213 million ($596 million) by 1965/66. In view of the surplus position of the economy and number of developments such as new industries that may or may not eventuate, it does not seem profitable to undertake a detailed projection of imports and exports.

Assuming that trade and financial remittances remain quite free, we may expect net imports to increase in accordance with the increase in government expenditures less private remittances abroad. Industries established to make items now imported should not have much effect on the net trade balance, although they may change the composition of imports. Of course, if soundly based industries processing natural gas or imported minerals are established, exports will increase more than imports of materials plus the remittance of earnings abroad. In this case Kuwait's normal imports may increase *pari passu* with the national income derived from sources other than oil, but one might expect the foreign exchange reserves also to increase.

Inflation and consequent balance of payments difficulties might occur only if government expenditures in the domestic economy plus bank credit expansion to the private sector were to exceed the foreign exchange made available to cover the demand for net imports (im-ports less exports) and foreign currency remittances. The Mission is aware of no plans for an expansion of developmental or current governmental expenditures, or of private demands on the banking systems, that make such an occurrence at all likely.

CHAPTER 7 *PUBLIC SECTOR INVESTMENT*

In this chapter we will first review the observations of the 1961 Mission on the Government's public works program and the steps subsequently taken by the Government in this field. We will then examine the amount now proposed for expenditure in 1963/64. Finally, we will suggest a program that appears reasonable through 1965/66. The Planning Board is beginning to prepare a detailed five-year plan scheduled to start two or three years from now. In this and the following chapter we make some observations on various long-range projects that may be of value to the Planning Board in preparing its five-year plan.

Administration and Planning

The Ministries of Public Works and of Electricity and Water are responsible for almost all public capital expenditures in Kuwait. The former executes all major construction projects except those involving power and water supply. Many of these projects are executed on behalf of other ministries (schools, hospitals, government buildings) but others are initiated by the Ministry of Public Works itself (roads, sewerage, airports). The Ministry puts them all together in a capital budget which is combined with the current operating budget of the Government by the Ministry of Finance and Industry. The same applies to the budget of the Ministry of Electricity and Water. However, this latter Ministry, unlike Public Works, actually operates the facilities it constructs. The operational responsibility of Public Works aside from construction, is largely confined to the maintenance of the works it builds and to the operation of a few facilities such as the Agricultural Experimental Farm.

The 1961 Mission felt that concentration of construction of major projects in the Ministry of Public Works was desirable since this should help to ensure that tenders are processed without preference and awards made to the best bidder. Better technical supervision would also be possible with this concentration. These observations still appear to be valid. Nor does it appear desirable to separate in different ministries the construction and maintenance functions as has been proposed.

Budgetary Procedures. The general features of budgetary procedures in Kuwait and the Mission's recommendations relating thereto are in Chapter 3. Here we discuss the budget as it pertains to the public investment program.

The annual budget for recurrent and maintenance works is prepared on the basis of the previous year's expenditure experience. For new works, for long-term projects and "unfinished work" (both major and minor) the cost estimates are made by PWD. If projects are not finished within the year, the unfinished work and any supplemental funds required must be covered in the succeeding year's budget. Unexpended funds are not automatically carried forward but have to be re-appropriated.

In reality the program is made up by compiling requests of the various departments. These requests are priced by PWD and passed upon by the Planning Board. The initial costing of the various items is likely to be inaccurate and subject to later revision. The order of priority often reflects pressure brought by the individual ministries. When the program is prepared, it is transmitted through the Planning Board to the Ministry of Finance and Industry. Subsequently, the Ministry sets a maximum allocation, and the Planning Board in consultation with Public Works recasts the program to fit the allocated amount. This method of across-the-board reduction without any real consultation between the budget-makers and the spending agencies does not make for the most effective use of public funds. It may, however, have been the only practical approach possible until interdepartmental machinery was established for effective coordination in budget-making and other general governmental operations, and, particularly, until a comprehensive longer-range development program is prepared.

The subject of maintenance expenditures deserves particular comment. At the present time it is practically impossible to identify clearly the total provisions of the budget for maintenance of completed works. Segments of maintenance costs are carried under different sections of the budget, materials under one section, wages and overtime under another, transport under still another and additional works under a fourth. Because the costs of maintenance will continue to increase annually as various works and installations are finished, it becomes an important segment of expenditure. It would be better if the budget contained a separate section titled Maintenance of Installations, with separate subsections for each general category of work such as roads, government buildings, schools, hospitals, parks, sewer systems and any other general area of responsibility. Under each of these general sections there should be a subsection showing the cost of labor, transport, overtime, materials and general expenses. Such an arrangement would also compel more detailed and thoughtful budget preparation. It would pull together into one sector of the budget the expenditures now provided in various sections and by identifying the total cost, indicate opportunity for reducing expenditure. By bringing these activities under constant control and review it should prevent the use of maintenance funds for miscellaneous and minor capital expenditures not planned or budgeted. At the same time it should help to assure that adequate funds are provided for maintenance, which is essential for economy in the over-all program.

Project Execution. After a request for a project is received and approved, the responsibility for all design, costing and execution devolves on the Ministry of Public Works. Public Works projects are carried out, in the main, by contract. Contracts are made as a result of public tenders, and large contracts are offered for international tenders. Performance bonds in the form of bank guarantees are provided by the tenderers with their proposal, and a performance bond, usually 10 per cent of the contract, is provided by the successful tenderer on signature of the contract. Non-Kuwaiti contractors are required to be sponsored by Kuwaitis.

Projects are designed partly by the staff of the Public Works Design Office and partly by private architects, engineers and firms. In the past, procedure was to engage private engineering firms by open tender. During the past few years attempts have been made to change this system and substitute the more normal negotiated agreement with firms of repute which base their fees on the internationally accepted scales. This is a more desirable procedure, providing adequate care is taken in negotiating the agreements.

Inspection of materials and control of construction are carried out by a considerable staff of engineers, technical assistants and foremen to supervise the contractors' work. The services of a research station are available for checking on the quality of materials. Contractors are not limited in any way as to source of materials, provided that such material agrees and complies with the terms of the specification. In the past the Government sometimes made purchases and then transferred materials to the contractors. The present day tendency is to avoid the purchase by the Government on behalf of the contractors. The construction equipment is normally supplied by the private contractor, but there are cases when government equipment is rented to the contractor.

Planning. When the 1961 Mission visited Kuwait, any planning activity on a formalized basis was the responsibility of the Development Board. This Agency, established in 1960, consisted of a President (now Minister), appointed by decree from among the members of the Supreme Council and six Kuwaiti-voting members from the private sector appointed by the Supreme Council (now the Council of Ministers). Non-voting members were the Chief Engineers of the Public Works Department and the Department of Electricity, Water and Gas. The President of the Public Works Department was President of the Board and, in reality, the Board was part of PWD. Although its terms of reference contained the instruction to plan large development schemes and phase the execution of such schemes, subject to the approval of the Supreme Council, its structure and the further description of its task in the Law put the major emphasis on detailed construction work; the Law did not mention the financial, economic and social aspects of a comprehensive development policy. The Board's principal drawback was lack of ministerial level representation and lack of an adequate secretariat. In practice it was referred to as a "construction board." Its limited scope and equipment prevented it from doing the research and planning badly needed for the formulation of a development plan, for coordinating the programs of the various departments and for establishing an order of priority within well defined financial limits.

The Mission therefore recommended that the Development Board should be basically altered, reorganized and restaffed so it could draw up a comprehensive development plan. Once prepared the Development Plan would be submitted to the Supreme Council and the Ruler. After approval of the Plan an Amiri Decree should be issued putting it into effect. The Plan would thus become a directive to the spending departments in preparing and executing projects and to the Department of Finance and Economy in the preparation of the annual budget. Any development program adopted should be reviewed not less frequently than once a year. The detailed recommendations of the 1961 Mission for the organization of the Planning Board were as follows:

It should have a President as Chairman who was not, at the same time, responsible for a major spending department. It would be appropriate if the Chairman of the Supreme Council were also Chairman of the Development Board. Its direct management should be entrusted to a full-time Deputy Chairman with the rank of Director General. It would be desirable to engage, at least temporarily, for assistance to the Chairman and Deputy Chairman, an outstanding economist, to give the Deputy Chairman an opportunity to study similar organizations in the region or elsewhere.

The Mission suggested that under the President the Board should have four private members, representative of different interests in the community, and appointed by the Supreme Council on nomination either by the President or by such bodies as the Municipal Council and the Chamber of Commerce. The Board also should have five official members, chosen from among the Presidents of the departments most concerned with development programs and policy. As the Board was not expected to convene frequently, it might usefully select from its membership a small Steering Committee that could meet more often with the President and/or the Deputy Chairman to discuss current matters, particularly during the first year or so.

The Secretary of the Board should be a senior official with financial and administrative competence of a high order. He should *not* have the title and rank of assistant, which would place him on a level with others of inferior responsibility. Among the units under him would be a small administrative secretariat to assist the Secretary and the Deputy Chairman. There should also be a public information section, to take care of the important matter of informing the public about the development plan and its progress.

The most important subdivision should be that for planning and reports, which should be placed directly under the Deputy Chairman, It should consist of a working group of five or six experts in different fields, such as a general economist, an industrial economist, a civil engineer, a town planner, experts on education and health, and a sociologist. Other specialists could be added *ad hoc* as the work required. They should be drawn, if possible, from various sectors of the administration, or on a temporary basis from outside. They should have the duty and the authority to consult others and to get into direct contact with government departments and services for information and advice. It would be their duty to formulate the draft of a development plan and to revise it periodically after its initial adoption by the Government. They would, of course, assist the Board in its discussion of such a draft and its subsequent adaptations.

Once a development plan was put into effect, it would be the further duty of this subdivision to follow and report upon its execution, without, however, assuming any authority over the departments and services to which the execution would be assigned. Although the working group would need some technical personnel, it was never intended to have any direct responsibility for the execution of the plan itself. It would regularly draw up progress reports and offer comments and recommendations as and when needed.

The Mission recommended another subdivision to collect and organize the statistical material needed for the development plan, and if possible, to lay the foundation for a Central Statistical Office. Statistics are as yet but poorly developed in Kuwait and responsibility for them is badly scattered among many departments and offices. If a Central Statistical Office were established elsewhere, the statistics division of the Development Board would concentrate on collecting the statistics needed in preparing the development program. The staff of the statistical subdivision should be determined by the requirements of the planning and reporting functions; it should be directed by a statistical expert who in the first instance probably would have to be recruited abroad.

A fourth subdivision seemed desirable for supplementary research that could not be performed by the departments. Such research would probably mainly be of an economic and sociological nature, but it could also be helpful in studying developmental organizations and results elsewhere, and might concentrate on special problems such as survey of natural resources.

On August 14, 1962, the present Planning Board was established (Decree No. 56 of 1962) along substantially the lines (taking account of the intervening constitutional changes) that the 1961 Mission had suggested, except that its functions are rather more extensive than the Mission had contemplated. The Prime Minister is Chairman and the Minister of Finance and Industry, Deputy Chairman. Its responsibility is the "formulation of the general economic and social policy, and the establishment of development programs and the supervision of their implementation." Up to the present time its more important function has been the review of the 1963/64 capital budget. Since the Board has broad responsibilities for economic affairs not directly related to long-range planning, it has been meeting frequently on a broad range of subjects, thus becoming, in effect, an economic committee of the Council of Ministers. The Mission was informed that the private members are very influential. Since the Director General is just now in the process of recruiting a staff, it is too early to judge the quality of the planning job that the Board will accomplish. It will, of course, require the close cooperation of the various ministries—particularly the Ministry of Public Works and the Ministry of Electricity and Water, to which the staff of the Board will have to look for engineering assistance. The Board has been established at an appropriately high level in the Government, and should be a useful instrument for formulating and coordinating economic policies. The economy is of such a comparatively small size that the comprehensiveness of the Board's functions should prove to be manageable.

Public Works Expenditures 1961/62–1963/64

The 1961 Mission recommended that 28 per cent of total revenues of the State be used for domestic public development expenditures during the five years 1961/62–1965/66. This would have involved an average annual outlay of about KD 57 million a year, KD 44 million for public works and about KD 13 million a year of public investment in or for the private sector. Of the KD 220 million that this program would have provided for the public sector, it was estimated that KD 70 million would be required for the overhead and administrative expenditures of the Ministry of Public Works and about KD 150 million for strictly project expenditures, or KD 30 million a year. At that time the then Public Works Department was projecting, in the 1961/62 budget, project outlays averaging about KD 39 million a year over the three years 1961/62–1963/64, exclusive of the capital outlays of the Ministry of Electricity and Water. No official projection was then available of expenditures of the Ministry or of possible public investment in the private sector.

Following the 1961 Mission's visit, actual allocations for public works in the annual budgets for 1961/62 and 1962/63 were sharply reduced. This was partly because of delays in the start of projects due to technical reasons and probably also because of the crisis which developed with Iraq.[1] In any event, the final budget allocations for PWD projects in those two years totaled only KD 43.46 million (about half the amount originally proposed) and actual expenditures were only KD 38.64 million. In addition, the Electricity and Water Department spent KD 14.45 million. Thus, total capital expenditures in 1961/62 and 1962/63 were about KD 53 million, or KD 7 million a year less than the rate the Mission had suggested. The breakdown of these expenditures and a comparison with the amounts allocated is

---

[1] The 1961 Mission had noted "there is evidence that the execution of such a program (about KD 118 million) within the three-year period is beyond the present capacity of the technical staff of the Public Works Department and that the phasing should extend at least over a four or five-year period."

shown in Statistical Annex Table VII. Development expenditures in the public sector were about 19 per cent of total public revenues as compared with the 22 per cent suggested by the Mission. They were at about the same level as in 1960/61 and considerably lower than in the boom year 1959/60. Nor did the substantial investments which the Mission thought might be made by the State in or for the private sector materialize on any substantial scale.

It seems probable that development expenditures will increase substantially in 1963/64 and may well exceed the KD 30 million a year suggested as a norm for the five year period 1961/62–1965/66. Budget allocations for capital investment are over KD 42 million, KD 12 million higher than in 1962/63. Several substantial projects and programs which have been moving quite slowly up to now (airport, housing for low income families) are expected to require much more during the current year. Assuming that the 1963/64 appropriation is substantially spent, it is possible to compare the expenditures and allocations during the first three years of the five-year period with the totals suggested by the 1961 Mission.

Thus, about 30 per cent of the five-year program envisaged by the 1961 Mission was completed during the first two years. This compared with about 35 per cent which appeared possible two years ago. Part of this shortfall, however, was because of a re-examination, suggested by the Mission, of the airport project. The remainder appears to have been largely due to delays in getting the low-income housing program under way and in starting work on the new Mubarak Hospital. All three of these parts of the program are expected to result in substantial expenditures during the next three years. Expenditures totaling about KD 91 million seem to be needed from 1963/64 through 1965/66 for the Ministry of Public Works.[2] This, together with the KD 45.5 million spent during the last two years (excluding power, which was not included in the Mission forecast) would total about KD 136 million, leaving a shortfall of KD 14 million below the Mission's estimate. If housing, sewerage and water facilities had been installed as needed, this gap would probably have been closed. Therefore, it may be concluded that the 1961 Mission's estimate of public capital expenditures of about KD 150 million was a fairly accurate calculation of the needs of Kuwait (apart from the power program) during the five-year period in question.

[2] According to the projections in the 1963/64 budget of the Ministry, expenditures may be as follows: 1963/64–KD 35.87 million; 1964/65–KD 32.57 million; and 1965/66–KD 23.04 million for the projects already in the program.

TABLE 15: Investment in the Public Sector   (Million KD)

	(1)	(2)	(3)	(4)	(5)
Project or Program	Expenditure Suggested by 1961 Mission –1961/62 to 1965/66	Actual Expenditure in 1961/62 & 1962/63	Per cent (2) of (1)	Amount Required to Complete Current Projects [a]	1963/64 Budget
Airport	13.00	1.00	8	13.00	3.60
Port	4.00	2.00	50	6.35 [d]	1.25
Roads and Streets	24.00 [e]	8.23	34	15.07 [e]	3.60
Housing	15.00	1.19	8	4.60 [e]	2.60
Education Facilities	19.00	5.80	27	24.48	9.95
Health Facilities	18.00	2.00	11	8.29	1.67
Power and Water Supply	19.00 [f]	14.20	36 [b]	n.a.	10.77
Sewers and Drainage	16.00	3.60	23	9.00	2.60
Government Buildings	15.00	11.10	74	9.20	2.80
Other	7.00	8.90	127	0.59	3.90
Total	150.00	58.02	30 [b]	90.58	42.74

[a] Based on 1963/64 budget presentation to the Planning Board by Minister of Public Works.

[b] Mission estimate did not contain provision for additional power facilities. Therefore, per cent in column (3) is for expenditure on water only.

[e] Includes KD 7 million for the corniche (water front improvement) at Kuwait City now estimated to cost about KD 12 million.

[d] Port at Shuaibh.

[e] Includes recreational facilities in housing areas.

[f] Does not include KD 6.87 million for electric power.

Source: Ministries of Public Works and Electricity and Water.

Since important new developments have occurred in housing and water supply since 1961, these two programs will be discussed in some detail. The comments of the 1961 Mission on some other sectors of the program, revised as need be, are then summarized.

Housing

The main purpose of a government house construction program in Kuwait is to provide houses for the lower-income Kuwaitis and the Bedouin. The rapid growth of population and the congestion now prevalent in the lower-income residential areas have prompted an acceleration of this program.[3] The Social Affairs Ministry, which has charge of the low-income housing program, informed the 1963 Mission that 4,035 houses had already been built, of which 276 remain to be turned over to their purchasers during the current year.[4] New applications for 4,000 more low-income houses are said to be on file at present. Accordingly, a plan has been drawn up for the construction of 10,000 new houses in the coming eight years, of which 6,000 would be for low-income Kuwaitis and 4,000 for Bedouins. Most of the latter are very inadequately housed in shacks on the outskirts of Kuwait City. The cost of this program has apparently not been included in column (4) of Table 15 above.

Government-built houses are made available on very generous terms.[5] In the first place "low-income" persons are defined as those whose monthly incomes do not exceed KD 150 ($420) a month, a fairly high income even by Kuwait standards. Secondly, payment is made over 25 years without interest; and payments apparently may be waived for reasons of poverty, or death of or accident to the head of the family. Houses may not be transferred outside the family, however—a stipulation apparently aimed at limiting the advantages of the program to Kuwaiti nationals. The applicant, in addition to meeting the income qualification, must be able to demonstrate the inadequacy of his present housing.

[3] According to a sample drawn from the 1961 population census, the number of persons per room varied with the size of the house. For owner-occupied dwellings it was five to seven persons (depending on location) for one-room houses but decreased to 2.3–2.9 persons per room for three-room houses. Rented and employer-supplied housing showed a somewhat lower number per room for the large dwellings.

[4] At least four ministries are involved in the housing program. These are:
1) *Municipality*—which licenses and supervises private construction and procures the land on which the government-constructed houses are built.
2) *Social Affairs*—which by Decree No. 2 of 1962 is responsible for the distribution of the government-constructed houses and collecting the payments from the owners.
3) *Public Works*—which constructs and maintains the houses.
4) *Credit Bank*—which has a housing program of its own for low-income government employees.

[5] The two types of low-income houses at present being built are known as the western type and the Kuwait type. A typical house consists of a plot of 500 square meters with a house with ground dimensions of 120 square meters. The cost varies between KD 4,500 and KD 5,250 per unit without the cost of land. The house consists of three main rooms, a large kitchen, a shower and a water closet. Facilities included in this house consist of electrical installation, water supply and sewerage disposal. The water supply provides for a dual distribution system for brackish and potable water.

The cost of street development, storm sewers and ultimate sanitary sewer systems are not charges against the cost of the individual housing units. The Mission was told that although some low-income housing has been occupied for as much as four years, the Government was not yet collecting the payments.

In general, the low-income housing program has commendable objectives and meets a pressing need. However, the following comments seem to be in order:

1) Limiting the benefits of the program to Kuwaitis seems unnecessarily restrictive. Persons who have resided in Kuwait for two or three years, say, are gainfully employed in jobs of economic value to the State, and have brought their families there, should also be allowed to participate in the program. We are aware that government-owned housing is provided to foreign contractors and civil servants above a certain salary grade, but this does not take care of the lower-income persons, particularly those working in the private sector on whom the development of the economy so largely depends. From our observations, employer-furnished housing at industrial establistments is usually quite inferior, and, in any case, is not suitable for employees with families in Kuwait.

2) The financial terms on which the houses are provided are unnecessarily generous, and are in strong contrast to the high rents paid by those who cannot participate in the program.

3) The administration of the program is in too many hands. In addition to the agencies mentioned above, there is a housing committee of citizens which determines priorities in distributing the houses, hears complaints, and so forth. This would seem to leave the way open for personal favoritism and perhaps arbitrary and inconsistent action. It was not clear to the Mission, either, why the Credit Bank, the main business of which should be to make loans for industrial projects, should have a housing program of its own.

4) The planning of the program seems to have been inadequate. Plans for public housing at the present time are not based on any survey of existing housing nor are they related to any kind of long-term plan. (The explanation given for this is that the need has been such that careful, long-term projection of requirements has seemed unnecessary.) This has led to a program

based entirely upon expediency and unrelated to the availability of utilities.

The location of this housing deserves a word of credit, however, for it is not segregated in one large area but reasonably well distributed through the entire community where space was either available or could be obtained by land purchase. Future housing programs, however, should be preceded by careful population studies, condition surveys of existing housing to determine what is sub-standard, and assessment of requirements for future municipal development programs. The Mission was glad to note that the housing requirements for the villagers and Bedouins are receiving attention.

Water

Requirements for Potable Water. Present production capacity of 6 million gallons a day of distilled water, and the construction of a pipeline from the Raudhatain water field in northern Kuwait to Kuwait City, appear to assure an adequate municipal supply for the next few years. Certainly this will be true if the capacity of the distillation plant is increased by the proposed 2 million gallons per day. This would allow for a considerable increase in the population of the urban area and still provide a daily potable water supply of about 35 gallons per person. Without taking into consideration water to be used for irrigation, it is estimated that an average consumption for a summer day of 35 gallons per capita is sufficient for a municipal water supply in Kuwait City. Consumption may reach higher levels after the Shatt-al-Arab waters become available and the water distribution scheme is carried out. For additional amounts required for irrigation, industry, or extensive watering of gardens, brackish water may be used, but of course fresh water would be far better.

The above considerations concern only the water supply problems of Kuwait City. Ahmadi has an adequate water supply, but there is a balance of at least 30,000 people in Kuwait who need a good water supply. Assuming the same rate of consumption as Kuwait City, this will require about 1 million gallons a day. Most of this population is toward the north along the road to Basra and southeast toward the coastline. Water can be provided for the first of these areas from the Raudhatain source.

Water Development. We may thus conclude that Kuwait can provide itself with adequate water for normal municipal uses from sources of the type now being used. Everyone to whom the Mission spoke, however, felt that development of vegetation is of utmost importance to assuage the harshness of the climate. Apart from the possibility of providing fresher food and vegetables, the presence of greenery and shade in the desert would make Kuwait an immeasurably more pleasant place in which to live. In addition, plants would hold the soil together and reduce the severity of the summer sandstorms. Agriculture might also employ some of the unskilled workers who will become redundant when the construction program tapers off. A detailed study of the related technical and economic problems will be required, however, taking into account the cost of importing vegetables by specially adapted trucks. The Government is well aware of this need.

Although there are drainage problems connected with the impervious layer of soil ("gatch"), the main problem of agriculture is the provision of an adequate supply of water for irrigation, plus possibly some enrichment of the soil with readily available fertilizers. There are three possible sources of brackish and three of sweet water. More detailed consideration is given to exploration and exploitation of water sources in Appendix 2.

a) Brackish Sources

Proposed Sewerage System for Kuwait City. Invitations to tender for a modern sewage disposal plant in the City of Kuwait have already been issued. The effluent water will be a mixture of brackish and fresh water. The dissolved solids content will, of course, depend on the proportions entering sewage. A reasonable figure to use in calculations would be 3,000 parts per million of dissolved salts. Under ideal conditions, water containing 2,000 parts per million of dissolved salts may be used for irrigation; and for some crops such as alfalfa, water containing as much as 3,000 parts per million might be used. The regular use of sewage effluent for irrigation, however, will involve either some mixing with sweet water or leaching with sweet water at intervals. Otherwise, salination of the soil will occur. Leaching would appear to be more economical of sweet water.

The advantage of using the sewage effluent water is that it would be produced where land could be cultivated near the city. This water should not be used for irrigation of vegetables particularly those to be eaten raw. The safest use is for growing animal feed stuffs.

Water from Damman Formation, Southwest Kuwait. The second source, the Damman formation and related water in southwestern

Kuwait could be large (see Chapter 2). Water tested by the Kuwait Oil Company indicates that a water supply could be developed which would contain about 2,000 parts per million of dissolved salts. This is suitable for irrigation given good drainage and irrigation practice (see insert on isosalinity Map 1). It seems likely that water could be piped to Kuwait City for 87 fils per 1,000 gallons.

If, instead of piping irrigation water to the environs of Kuwait City, a small agricultural community with modern facilities were developed in the southwestern corner of Kuwait, the project would have the following advantages:

1) The soil is more suitable for agriculture than around Kuwait City.
2) It should assist in settling the nomadic and semi-nomadic people.
3) It would save the cost of piping water to Kuwait City, and water costing only about 47 fils (13¢) per 1,000 gallons might be obtained.

All this development naturally depends on successful water exploration in this area.

Sulaibiya Wells. The wells at Sulaibiya, just southwest of Kuwait City, are the sole source of brackish water at present. Production capacity could be increased from the present 6.5 million gallons per day, to 18 or 20 million gallons a day; but the solid content is high, being some 4,000 parts per million.

b) Sweet Water Sources

Shatt-al-Arab Scheme. The use of water from the Shatt-al-Arab requires an agreement with the Iraq Government; an agreement has been concluded which gives Kuwait the right to draw 120 million gallons a day. The scheme of pumping 100 million gallons per day to the vicinity of Kuwait City as examined by Sir Alexander Gibb and Partners in 1954 envisaged a cost of about 29 fils (8¢) per 1,000 gallons if capital cost of the original plant is not charged; with the capital cost included, the cost would be about 68 fils (19¢). Gibb estimated that perhaps 5 per cent of the total discharge of the Shatt-al-Arab would be used, based on a minimum flow of the river of 120 cubic meters per second. New developments—an excellent access road, closer sources of natural gas, facilities developed for Raudhatain—might well tend to reduce the cost estimates.

More recent flood control, drainage and irrigation schemes in the Tigris-Euphrates Basin possibly would have an effect of decreasing flow and causing a further invasion of brackish and sea water upstream toward the proposed intake of the pipeline at Basra. Hence, these features would have to be re-examined. In addition, the share which the Government of Iraq would bear of installation costs and the cost of water to Kuwait would have to be negotiated.

Raudhatain Source. A check recently carried out shows that the sweet water foundation at the Raudhatain and adjoining fields may support a rate of pumping of 5 million gallons throughout most of the year. At this rate, the field is expected to last 20 years. So far, only some 2–3 million gallons per day have been taken. This fresh water should be used for domestic purposes only, or kept as a safety factor if, for example, the Shatt Scheme were to be implemented.

There are possibilities that fresh water may be found in other locations such as the Dibdibba, or more probably in northern or western Kuwait. Costs should be comparable to the above estimates for the Damman formation.

Desalination. Distilled water now costs 660 fils ($1.85) per 1,000 gallons to produce (see Statistical Annex Table VIII). This, however, is based on an average daily production of only 4,148,000 gallons (average 1962/63), whereas the possible production is more than 6 million gallons. In addition, the cost involves the old, less efficient and more expensive plant. If 6 million gallons a day were produced with present equipment, the cost would be reduced to about 473 fils per 1,000 gallons. In the new installation yielding 2 million gallons per day, the cost would be about 269 fils per 1,000 gallons. This could well be reduced to less than 200 fils (56¢) for a really big installation. However, even at the calculated rate of 269 fils, distilled water mixed 50/50 with brackish water at, say, 75 fils per 1,000 gallons, would produce water at 172 fils (48¢) per 1,000 gallons. Water at this price may be economical to use for growing certain kinds of vegetables.

In plants where fuel costs are not negligible, freezing or electro-dialysis of brackish water are probably more economical than distillation. Distillation, especially as it can use sea water rather than brackish water, may well be the most economical in Kuwait. Nevertheless, testing the two experimental electrodialysis plants already delivered in the search for cheaper methods of producing fresh water is well worthwhile.

Where electric power and distilled water are both required, the most economical arrangement is to use the exhaust from passout turbogenerators as the steam supply for condensation into distilled water. This has been difficult in the past in Kuwait owing to small storage capacity for water. The plants have been installed with water and power production in separate units. With use of water for irrigation, power and water production could be tied together once more. We recommend that the capital and operating costs should be looked into very closely. If, however, the decision is to continue the policy of separate units, then the generation of power by gas turbines rather than by steam turbo-alternators should be considered. This may save substantially in both capital and operating costs, but would have to be weighed against other considerations, such as the consequences of the possible breakdown of a large unit.

Other Projects

Other items in the Kuwait Public Works Program include almost every major type of public investment project: roads, streets, drainage, schools, hospitals, mosques, public buildings, PTT facilities, air transportation facilities, port facilities, urban redevelopment and an agricultural experiment station. Only the more important are mentioned here. Education and health facilities are discussed in Chapters 9 and 10.

Airport. This is the largest single Public Works project now under way; its estimated cost is KD 14.25 million. According to the expenditure projections of the Ministry of Public Works, the unexpended balance of KD 13 million (as of April 1, 1963) will be disbursed over the next three years, constituting about 14 per cent of public sector expenditures on long-range projects during that period.

With the physical expansion of Kuwait, the need for relocating and expanding airport facilities became apparent in 1955. The Development Board agreed to the proposed site south of the City at that time. In December 1957, it was decided that the PWD would do the construction. The airport was to be built to specifications for an International Class "A" airport able to handle the largest jet commercial aircraft. The design of the airport was put to international tender, and on May 26, 1958, the Development Board approved the awarding of the design and supervision of construction to Messrs. Frederick S. Snow and Partners of England.

In February 1960, a decision was taken to construct two runways, one temporary and the other permanent, as soon as possible. The decision to construct a temporary runway was taken because the permanent airport was not expected to be ready till 1963, and it was considered necessary to move the airport from its old site before that time for reasons of safety and also because the area was needed for higher priority uses. Following the completion of the permanent runway and supporting facilities, the "temporary" facilities were to be turned over to the military.

The 1961 Mission had some doubts as to the need for what amounts to two airports alongside each other. One runway of the dimensions envisaged in the original plans appeared adequate. Furthermore, what started out to be an inexpensive interim runway with temporary supporting buildings and facilities, in fact, became a complete airport in itself, capable of accepting all but the largest jets and limited in this respect only because the runway is 2,400 meters in length as compared to 3,400 meters for the permanent runway.

Following the Mission's visit the project was re-examined. It has now been decided to proceed with the second runway. However, the terminal buildings that were constructed for the first stage have been improved and will be used for the permanent airport, effecting considerable savings.

Ports. Kuwait has a fine seaport at Kuwait City, and another port is being planned in the new industrial area of Shuaibha. The 1961 Mission noted that import data disclose that approximately one-half of the present inbound tonnage is material to support the expanded public and private construction program now being executed. Of this tonnage, about 50 per cent is one commodity, cement. Since the development of the port area, particularly the warehouse section, is predicated on tonnages which are the result of this expanded construction program, the ultimate development may be substantially in excess of any normal requirement. Establishment of a free port might give rise to some increase in traffic; but it is well to remember that the present tariff is only 4 per cent, and that eliminating it would not necessarily greatly enhance Kuwait's already important role as a port of transit. For this reason it would seem prudent that the development program be restudied to make certain that the port is not in fact being overbuilt. This observation may be particularly pertinent if the present plan to erect a cement plant is carried out.

Roads and Streets. The main road network from Kuwait City north to Basra and south to Ahmadi has been completed. The present program consists largely of widening and resurfacing existing roads and paving the city streets. Extensive repaving probably will be needed when the installation of the new sewer network is completed. Sidewalks are lacking on many important streets in the City and should be constructed.

Telephones. Kuwait is short of adequate telephone facilities with only about 18,500 instruments (6,000 exchange lines). A ten-year plan is now before the Council of Ministers for 40,000 lines and probably about 130,000 instruments. The program is expected to cost about KD 10 million. Since the backlog of applications for instruments is now estimated at about 8,000 and new applications are about 1,500 a year, the size of the long-range program does not seem unreasonable. Heavy annual capital expenditures will start in 1964/65 (estimated at about KD 3.7 million in that year) but may decline in the later years of the program. At present, different flat basic rates are charged for commercial and residential use. The service is very cheap and will have to be increased if the system is to pay its way.

Appraisal of the Program

The public works program unquestionably would have benefited from more thorough and systematic planning. This not only would have reduced its cost but also would have produced greater benefits to the people of Kuwait. For example, such elementary and basic needs of modern urban living as piped water supply and sewerage disposal are only now being installed in Kuwait City, even though great boulevards, some very elaborate public buildings and palatial private residences have long since been in evidence. Also (perhaps owing to the abundance of motor vehicles), sidewalks are scarce and public transportation (except rather high-fare taxis) is not yet available. However, the Mission understands that a company has now been organized to provide bus transportation. The low-income housing program has also been slow to get under way and is now designed only for Kuwaiti citizens. On a more detailed point, the 1961 Mission observed that construction techniques were often rather slipshod, particularly in concrete work, and that the results might not be very durable. However, we are now informed that this is no longer true.

Despite shortcomings, the general results of the Public Works Program are indeed impressive. Great care and expense has been devoted to high-priority needs such as distilled water production, the seaport, hospitals and schools. The latter are probably among the best in the world from the physical standpoint.

The concentration of responsibility for the major construction projects in the Ministry of Public Works is sound, but the technical staff of that Ministry should be strengthened further in order to carry out the program on an orderly annual basis. The quality of the design and construction work would inevitably benefit.

There are also a substantial number of desirable public works not yet estimated for cost nor incorporated in the program. Examples are water exploration and possible development for a modest amount of irrigated agriculture, village development (housing, streets and sanitation) and further reconstruction of the old city. In the rephasing of the present program, long-term projects, new works and any projects not yet programmed (as noted above) should be reviewed together by the Planning Board. Also, the Public Works Program should be companion to and not at the expense of potential productive industrial development, which should have first call on the labor force and the technical capacity of the population. Public works could be used to support and maintain a uniform level of economic growth.

CHAPTER **8** *PRODUCTION POSSIBILITIES*

Industry

In most countries, industries have grown naturally from the exploitation of diverse indigenous raw materials or because of a cheap or technically highly competent work force. In Kuwait, however, industrialization must be based on some negative elements, namely, lack of alternative opportunities in agriculture and the Government's redundant work force, as well as such positive factors as plentiful oil and gas resources and cheap and abundant capital. Since public policy in Kuwait is to encourage gainful employment, and since some industrial investment is already occurring, the Mission has attempted to appraise the situation with a view to suggesting what further developments should receive government encouragement and support. As already noted, the economic costs of production may be less than the monetary costs calculated at going wage rates, and thus some subsidization may be justified.

Prospects for Export Industries

The availability of cheap capital provides a *prima facie* argument for capital-intensive industries. Those based on petroleum or natural gas are likely to fall in this category. However, the modern tendency is to build industries based on petroleum products near the center of demand rather than the source of supply. For this reason it is usually preferable to export the crude oil rather than the refined products. Since natural gas cannot be readily exported and as it is in plentiful supply it constitutes the most attractive raw material for use in Kuwait.[1]

[1] At present, Kuwait is exporting liquefied petroleum gas (LPG). Refinery gas produced in Kuwait contains a high proportion of propane and butane. This is liquefied, added to liquefied butane and propane obtained from the atmospheric gas at the gathering centers, and piped to the refinery. The liquid is fractionated and the propane and butane separated. The butane commands a ready sale as "bottled gas". The propane is not so readily marketable, as it has to be stored under considerable pressure to remain liquid. The propane could, however, serve as the basis of petrochemical manufacture as the starting point for propane and propylane derivative. The KOC have a contract to supply Japan with 300 tons of liquid gas per day, and bottled gas has a ready sale for domestic use in Kuwait.

113

Natural Gas. The present occurrence and collection of natural gas were described in Chapter 4. Because large quantities are flared off in the fields, the general assumption is that supplies are virtually unlimited. New processes tend to be specified with a moderate capital cost rather than a high thermal efficiency. This choice has consciously been made in the cases of the proposed cement plant and oil refinery. It is of utmost importance to review the surplus of gas available so that it may be used to the best advantage.

The over-all recovery of gas is directly proportional to the crude oil brought to the surface but, as the efficiency of the separation falls with increasing throughput, a smaller proportion of high pressure gas is recovered at high productions than at low. KOC estimates that, at current rates of oil production, the total gas available from the Burgan field at all pressures is 980 million cu. ft. per day. Although there may be some gas from offshore wells, this is likely to be little and expensive to recover and use. Present usage is about 301 million cu. ft. per day, and KOC has plans for using another 350 million cu. ft. for oil field operations. This leaves a surplus of 329 million cu. ft. for possible industrial projects.[2]

Uses of natural gas may be divided into three categories: (*a*) chemical raw material; (*b*) reducing agent; and (*c*) fuel.

a) Chemical raw material. It is technically possible to make every organic chemical (of which there are well over 1,000 in commercial production) from natural gas. On the other hand, every chemical so produced also may be produced from alternative sources such as coal or from fermentation of natural products. Whether petroleum or alternative sources are more economic depends on the particular product and upon the situation and circumstances of the proposed factory.

It appears likely that conditions in future will increasingly favor the production of organic chemicals from petroleum sources. Such sources have the advantage of relatively stable prices. In addition, many alternative sources are also sources of food, which, with expanding world population, will be required for human consumption.

---

[2] Owing to limited storage capacity for oil, considerable fluctuations in availability of gas are inevitable. If, for example, tankers cannot be brought alongside the pier for two or three days due to high seas, then oil production must be temporarily cut back. This will reduce the flow of gas. At present, this is no problem as demand is so much less than supply. If nearly all of the gas were used, however, an agreement would have to be reached with the KOC to suspend or reduce injection (oil field use) when production rates fall, to keep the new industries in operation.

As the American petrochemical industry is far bigger, both in quantity and variety, than in any other country, we have surveyed the chemicals currently in production in the United States. Sources list 119 chemicals derived directly from natural gases and 57 others produced from other petroleum sources.

The choice of a product is thus broad and difficult. A factor to be considered is that many processes are patented, and manufacturing royalties can amount to 10 per cent or 15 per cent of the total cost. This consideration is important when the owner of the patent is usually the competitor. In addition, technological improvements are taking place so rapidly that a chemical at present in good demand may be partly or totally superseded by a superior one in the near future. Furthermore, certain chemical companies hold a commanding position in their special fields and another company breaking in is liable to have to do so at prices considerably below world market prices.

For these reasons, the petrochemical industries have been organized as follows: The oil company (either by ownership of natural gas or by operation of a refinery) produces basic raw materials or possibly some of the simpler intermediates. Then companies formed jointly by a chemical company and the oil company are grouped close to the oil field or refinery. These convert the intermediates into the final product which is marketed by the chemical company through its established sales organizations.

This type of organization not only copes with the selling problem but also promotes a high level of research and development. The diversified and extensive nature of the plant, moreover, enables it to be switched from one product to another with the minimum expense.

The 1961 Mission recommended that, before entering the petrochemical field, a general decision should be taken by the Government whether to manufacture the final product or intermediates. The advantage of the final product is that profit margins tend to be higher because overheads may be somewhat lower in relation to gross sales. However, advantages of producing intermediates are:

1) As one intermediate can be used to produce several final products, there is not the same chance that an installation will be made obsolete by an improved product.

2) As the fuel and power content of an intermediate is higher, a bigger financial advantage lies where there is cheap fuel.

3) Smaller research, development and technical staffs are required.

4) Arrangements can be made more easily with existing chemical companies for finishing and marketing the products.

5) With establishment of an intermediate manufacturing plant, development into final products is easier as experience is gained both in production and marketing.

For these reasons, we believe that plant manufacturing intermediates would have a far greater chance of success in Kuwait than one going all the way to the final product.

There are certain intermediate chemicals of almost universal application which are marketed on a world scale. These include such products as acetone, ammonium fertilizers, carbon tetrachloride, ethyl alcohol, methyl alcohol, formaldehyde. The other intermediates have a more limited application and hence would be tied to sales to specific chemical companies.

Fertilizers. All artificial fertilizers are essentially sources of potassium, phosphorous or nitrogen. A country such as Kuwait, which has cheap power but no sources of potassium or phosphorous, can only consider production of nitrogenous fertilizers. Nitrogen may be fixed either as ammonia or nitric acid to form ammonium salts (or urea) or nitrates. These fertilizers include ammonium sulphate, ammonium phosphate, urea, calcium ammonium nitrate, potassium nitrate. All have uses at different seasons and for different crops. They are, however, all in world-wide demand, and this demand is increasing as population pressures increase and the necessity for higher food production grows.

The 1961 Mission considered that urea seemed the most promising for Kuwait. However, a more detailed appraisal was necessary. Since Kuwait does not have the staff with the necessary qualifications either to carry out negotiations and scrutinize proposals or to collaborate during the construction and running of any chemical industry, the Mission recommended that consultants of high standing be engaged.

The Government has followed the recommended procedure. After one unsuccessful start, it has recently signed an agreement with British Petroleum and Gulf to set up a factory at Shuaibh for the manufacture of urea and ammonium sulphate. A marketing organization is still to be formed.

Investigation of production costs and available markets showed that although urea is by far the most profitable fertilizer to produce in Kuwait, quantities would overwhelm the markets readily available. It was decided, therefore, to produce ammonium sulphate as well as urea. Importing sulphur from Iraq would improve the profitability of ammonium sulphate.

In another sector of the oil industry, the Kuwait National Petroleum Company is planning to build a refinery using the new hydrogenation process to produce a larger proportion of the lighter fractions. For this process, large quantities of natural gas will be required—up to 67 million cu.ft. per day according to the Company. The refinery will come on stream in two years and will produce about 83,000 barrels per day. This will consist of 67–69,000 barrels per day of middle distillate (for kerosene) and diesel fuel; 3,000 barrels per day of heavy fuel oil; and 11–13,000 barrels per day of naphthas (for gasoline). The gasoline will be used in Kuwait; the middle distillates will be exported to South Asia and Africa.

The refinery, fertilizer plant and associated power and water services will take a total of between 75 million and 114 million cu. ft. of natural gas per day, leaving an over-all surplus of 215 to 256 million cu.ft. per day. Thus a figure of 200 million cu.ft. may safely be taken as the gas available for additional projects.

b) Metallurgical Use of Gas. By passing a mixture of steam and natural gas over a catalyst, a powerful reducing gas is formed. This gas, a mixture of hydrogen and carbon monoxide, may be used in the reduction of metallic ores. As Kuwait has no mineral resources or local market, it would be necessary to import ore and export the metal.

The production of sponge or direct iron by catalyzed natural gas is most attractive in principle, since it would avoid the use of high grade coking coals and obviate investment in blast furnaces and coke ovens. Many processes and patents have been developed for this purpose. However, direct iron for steel-making has only been produced commercially in one plant in the world. This is in Mexico, and is producing some 500 tons of steel per day. Construction of a plant in Kuwait would have to be regarded as a pioneering project, and it would be necessary to carry out extensive trials of the ore it is proposed to use. Facilities for such testing are available, and tests should be carried out prior to undertaking an investment in Kuwait.

c) Gas as Fuel. Large quantities of fuel both for heating and for generating electrical power are used in the chemical and metal-lurgical industries. The only chemical plant at present in Kuwait is a small installation for producing chlorine and caustic soda, erected by the Ministry of Power and Water to supply chlorine for water purification. Electrolysis of sea water produces the chlorine and soda. The caustic soda is used on the home market or may be sold to KOC for refinery operation. If a soap factory is established, it will provide a ready outlet for the caustic soda.

A small amount of chlorine is used locally for sterilizing water, and more could be used in a local chemical industry. It is not economic to export it even after conversion to hydrochloric acid. Sodium, either as caustic soda or soda ash (anhydrous sodium carbonate), is too widely produced to make export an attractive proposition. Special circumstances, however, might render its production economic. For instance, if alumina were imported for reduction to aluminum, then soda ash could be returned in the same ships for use in extracting alumina from bauxite.

The sea provides a possible source of other chemicals. Apart from sodium and chlorine, the elements appearing in the biggest quantities are magnesium and bromine. Bromine is extracted by neutralizing sea water with acid and treating it with chlorine. Chlorine substitutes for the bromine, which is liberated as a gas. As the major use of bromine is in ethylene dibromide for use in tetraethyl lead, this would be technically attractive if associated with an industry producing ethylene. Marketing would present a problem as virtually all tetra-ethyl lead is produced by the Associated Ethyl Corporation (a subsidiary of Standard Oil).

Magnesium is produced by evaporation of sea water and precipitation of the magnesium chloride. The effluent from the water distillation plant would be a start in this process. The magnesium chloride is dehydrated and electrolyzed to metallic magnesium. Although uses of magnesium are growing yearly, there is, at present, more productive capacity than market. This is due to the construction of many plants during the war for aluminum-magnesium alloy production. We could not, therefore, recommend magnesium as an economic material to produce at present. There is no doubt that, as other construction materials become more expensive, uses of magnesium will expand and it might well be that in a few years' time, production of magnesium in Kuwait could become a profitable undertaking.

Aluminum is produced from alumina by electrolysis, and the main cost is for electric power. This power could be produced by generators driven by natural gas turbines. The saving in power costs, however, must be balanced against the cost of transporting alumina to Kuwait and hauling virtually all the aluminum out again. The Mission, nevertheless, feels that this is worth consideration as a possible future project.

Kuwait Light Distillate. In completing this summary of possible petroleum or gas-based industries, mention should be made of a product now partly wasted. This is Kuwait Light Distillate produced by the present KOC refinery. About half the production is surplus, and has to be injected into the ground. Construction of the new refinery will increase the surplus. This fraction contains 90 per cent hexanes and the rest pentanes. It is a valuable raw material for petrochemicals, as it may be made cyclic and dehydrogenated as a starting point for all the aromatic hydrocarbons. As with natural gas, the choice of products is extensive and a careful survey must be made of marketability. Establishment of a petrochemical complex based on natural gas should be given priority, but the possibility of using the distillate should not be overlooked. About 1 million tons a year of products that could be made from distillate are sold throughout the world.

Industrial Estate

In 1961, the Government had plans for establishing an industrial estate for heavy industries. These industries would need considerable quantities of gas and adjacent port facilities, and could well be noisy and odorous. It was therefore proposed to establish them some distance from Kuwait City. A suitable site had been chosen between the village of Shuaibha and Mina Abdullah. The Mission endorsed these plans, and progress has been made in laying out the estate.

Areas have been planned for the fertilizer plant and for the proposed refinery of the National Petroleum Company. A space has been left along the shore for any industry requiring bulk handling of solids. A combined power station and distillation plant is in the course of construction with outputs of 210 megawatts and 3,000,000 gallons of water per day. The Ministry of Power and Water is responsible for planning and placing contracts for this project and for the natural gas pipeline to the estate. The Port Authority will be responsible for all port and harbor installations as well as for running the port, while the Public Works Ministry will have responsibilities for such things as roads and drains.

It is proposed to set up an Industrial Estate Authority. This will be responsible to the Minister of Finance and Industry, the members of the Board being appointed by the Minister. These appointments should be for a reasonable time, say, five years, to give some freedom of action. The Board should include the Director General of the

Planning Board and perhaps the General Manager of the Credit Bank. The Board will, of course, be part time, but a permanent staff consisting of a qualified accountant to act as Secretary to the Board and head the accounts department would be provided. No technical staff is envisaged, consultants being appointed by the Board when required. It is important to define the relationship of the Board to the industries on the estate and the ministries providing the services.

The law setting up the Authority should include the following provisions:

a) The Ministries (Power and Water, Public Works, etc.) should provide their services at cost to the Authority (taken over, say, a five-year period) with a minimum overhead to cover direct technical supervision.[3]

b) The Authority should represent the factories on the estate in negotiations with the various official bodies in Kuwait. The ministries should bill the Authority for services, and the Authority should bill the individual factories. The electrical power, for example, should be charged to the Authority at an agreed rate, but may well be charged to the consumers at variable rates.

c) Finances for the Authority in the development stage would be from a budget appropriation as approved by the Planning Board. But, once running, the Authority should be self-supporting, and should require finance only for expansion and further development.

Financing Required for Export Industries

The investment required to exploit surplus natural gas will vary with the type of product chosen. The Mission has estimated that the capital cost would be over KD 30 million per 100 million cu.ft. of gas per day or, say, KD 100 million for the 300 million cu.ft. available. This does not include off-site capital costs such as electricity, sewage,

---

[3] In the event of a dispute over rates to be charged or over the quality of service given, the Ministry and the Authority should appoint a mutually acceptable firm of consultants to investigate the causes of the dispute and make recommendations for a solution. It should be stipulated in the law that appointment of the consultant will bind them to accept his findings. In the event of a mutually acceptable consultant not being found, the Council of Ministers should appoint one.

and waste disposal, which are included under public works in the previous chapter. Assuming the land is free, the cost of an industrial estate (including a simple quay for shipping) would be about KD 10 million. Workers' living accommodations would increase the total to about KD 20 million.

An aggregate investment of about KD 120 million, therefore, may be required during the next five years or so, not including investment in facilities to exploit the Kuwait Light Distillate, which might also take a substantial amount of capital. In estimating possible government investment in the private sector, we have assumed that to encourage private investment, the Government would provide the KD 20 million needed for the industrial estate and workers' housing. Of the remaining KD 100 million of industrial investment, we have assumed a government participation of about 60 per cent or roughly KD 60 million. Thus, a total of KD 80 million has been allocated in our projections for public investment summarized in Chapter 6.

Prospects for Domestically-orientated Industries

The small home market and the combination of high wage rates with low productivity are likely to prevent most labor-intensive industries from operating successfully unless they have government support. Local industries are likely to be able to compete only where natural protection exists. Natural protection may be afforded by such factors as high transport costs and the unique demand of the local market for a particular product. Exceptions to this general proposition will arise if a local manufacturer is unusually efficient or where he has a particularly good specialized design that meets local tastes.

In order to provide employment and to build up a skilled labor force, some domestic industries merit reasonable assistance and support. The Ministry of Finance and Industry recognizes this and is, at present, preparing a law for "The Regulation, Protection and Encouragement of Industry." The objectives of the draft law are good. It provides for tax exemptions (including exemption from customs duties for imports of raw materials and semi-finished components for a period of ten years), free assignment of land, and access by the sponsors to all information, data and reports on the industry in the Government's files. These benefits are of the type normally provided by countries desiring to encourage new industry. We believe they should be provided.

There are, however, three important provisions which require comment, since they might be enforced in a way that would produce undesirable results:

1) Registration and licensing of new industries, including the revoking of licenses, if certain conditions are not met.
2) The use of protective tariffs.
3) Possible prohibition or restriction of imports of foreign goods that might compete with domestically produced goods.

Registration and Licensing. Compulsory registration of new industries is desirable for statistical purposes and to ensure that the promoter has sound advice on the viability of his project. Also, it is prudent for a government credit agency to refuse loans if it considers that the market will be over-supplied. Any refusal to license a project because of a desire to protect existing industry, however, is undesirable, because it will remove any incentive for those industries to improve quality, reduce prices and improve service to the consumer. The industrial section of the Ministry of Finance and Industry intends, we know, to apply the provision liberally and allow industries to start even when the market appears to be already supplied. The existence of this provision in the law, however, will expose the Ministry to irresistible pressure from existing industries to prohibit the entrance of competition. We know of no instances where a compulsory licensing arrangement, as proposed in this law, has worked well in a free economy; and, with Kuwait's abundance of funds, the usual argument that licensing is needed to conserve capital does not apply. We recommend therefore that licensing should be deleted from the proposed law and that only compulsory registration be provided.

Import Tariffs. At present the Government gives considerable assistance to local industry by the provision of land at low rentals, cheap loan and equity capital, and cheap fuel. There is also the possibility of supplying low-cost power and facilities on the industrial estates. All these subsidize local industry to a substantial extent, and this type of government assistance could be extended if necessary. For instance, the Government could pay some or all of the salary of a foreign expert to run the plant for a number of years and provide special training facilities for the labor force. All these types of assistance are desirable, and can be channeled so that the quality and efficiency of local industry are improved. Industries which cannot be made profitable on this basis are probably not attractive anyway. Therefore, we do not feel that high protective tariffs should be used in Kuwait.

It is true, of course, that import tariffs are an internationally recognized instrument for encouraging home industry, particularly new industries. If a moderate tariff could be applied for, say, five years, during the time a new industry is getting established, training its labor force and establishing its product in the market, and then be removed, no objection should be made. It may be very difficult, however, to remove a tariff once imposed. If the Government decides to use tariffs, we feel that the rates should be written into law and should not be left to a committee. Rates should not exceed 20 per cent *ad valorem* and should lapse for each specific product after five years unless extended by law.

Prohibitions or Quantitative Restriction on Imports. We feel that these have no economic justification in Kuwait as, under international trade principles, they are justified only on balance of payments grounds.

Credit Bank

As an encouragement to industry, the Ministry of Finance and Industry set up the Credit Bank in October 1960. Previously, no specialized institutions providing industrial, real estate or other types of immediate or long-term credit, had operated in the public or private sector.[4] The private commercial banks do an orthodox banking business. The commercial (rather than industrial) nature of the Kuwait economy provides them with ample opportunities without going farther afield. The ease with which they can invest their funds abroad probably also encourages them to adhere to short-term financing.[5]

The salient features of the character and regulations of the new institution were as follows:

1) The capital of KD 7.5 million was entirely subscribed by the Government.

[4] As has been previously indicated, some government funds had been made available for joint public and private sector industrial and transportation ventures. This appears to have been done largely on an *ad hoc* basis.

[5] This is not to deny that some commercial bank credits may be used for industrial purposes, since usually a Kuwaiti industrialist is also a merchant, and the banks do not usually ask the purposes for which a borrower of sound credit proposes to use the proceeds of a loan. Nor do the banks appear to worry about the extension of credits beyond the term of normal commercial loans, although overdue loans are sometimes assessed at 7 per cent rather than 5 per cent interest.

2) The Bank may borrow from the Government, or from others against the guarantee of the Government, up to the extent of its subscribed capital, and may borrow beyond this limit with the sanction of the Ministry of Finance and Industry.

3) The Bank has a Board of Directors of seven members appointed for three-year terms ("automatically renewable") by the Minister of Finance and Industry. The Chairman of the Board is the General Manager of the Bank.

4) The Bank has an independent budget, but the employees are subject to civil service regulations.

5) The Bank's field of loan operations is extremely broad, both in respect to the purposes for which its funds may be used and the maturities on its loans. Real estate, industrial and agricultural loans may be made, each on a short, medium or long-term basis.[6]

6) Loans (of limited amounts) may be made to government workers, secured by their future salaries, termination benefits, etc.

7) Besides lending, the Bank is permitted to "establish companies . . . and participate in the capital of these companies."

8) Borrowers must be either individual Kuwaitis or business enterprises with majority Kuwaiti participation.

9) While the Board of Directors is left with broad powers concerning rates of interest and, within limits established by the loan regulations, the terms of lending, the decisions of the Board require validation by the Minister of Finance and Industry, who also issues the regulations under which the Bank operates and approves its annual budget.

Normally, it would appear preferable that such a large variety of lending operations not be concentrated in one institution. In particular, the loans to government employees require quite different policies and procedures from those applicable to industrial and agricultural loans. The same is also true, perhaps to a lesser extent, of housing loans. Even agricultural and industrial lending would normally be conducted through separate institutions, although in Kuwait, barring

[6] Industrial loans are to be primarily for the construction of factories or dormitories for workers. The Bank may lend up to 50 per cent of the value of factory buildings and machinery, and up to 30 per cent of the value of dormitory lands and buildings. No more than 10 per cent of the financial resources of the Bank may be lent to a single borrower. The importance of the industries to the economy as well as the need for funds is to be taken into account.

the development of new water resources, agricultural loans are not likely to assume sufficient importance to warrant such a move. We think it unnecessary to suggest at this time an institutional separation of consumer and housing credit from industrial and agricultural lending. However, it is important that these diverse activities be handled by separate departments within the Bank and, for the most part, by different loan analysts.

The Mission has the following comments on the charter of the Bank:

a) The charter permits the Bank to acquire and exploit real estate. Such acquisition of property should be incidental to regular banking functions; the Bank should not engage in the real estate business as such.

b) In the final analysis, the management of the Bank is under the control of the Minister of Finance and Industry (Article 15). While in practice the Minister may not wish to exercise all his powers, he now has a veto over all loans, and the Board of Directors is placed in an advisory rather than a policy-making role. We do not feel that this veto is necessary.

c) The Chairman of the Board of Directors is the General Manager of the Bank. This gives him the dual role of supervising the day-to-day operations of the Bank, including the preparation of loan recommendations to the Board, and leading the Board in its consideration of such loans. While it is necessary that the Chief Executive Officer of the Bank present loan proposals to the Board and, if necessary, defend them, it is not desirable that he should have a vote which may be decisive in approving them. The separation of the positions of Chairman of the Board of Directors and General Manager would be desirable; the General Manager might be a member of the Board *ex officio*.

d) Neither the charter nor the regulations which have been issued under it discuss the technical services that might be provided by the Bank to its clients and other prospective Kuwaiti industrialists. These could be its most important functions.

A small section has been set up in the Bank, consisting of one accountant and one engineer, seconded from the Industrial and Commercial Finance Corporation of London, and a Kuwaiti. The function of this section is to examine the commercial and technical viability of applications for loans. A summary of the applications and loans granted so far is given in Statistical Annex Table IX, indicating the small scale of its operations to date.

However, the Industries Section of the Ministry of Finance and Industry is also establishing a unit to advise promoters of industrial enterprises, and also, presumably, to examine new possibilities and try to interest industrialists in them. There seems a great possibility of overlapping functions here; the Ministry should concern itself with policy rather than operations. The Mission recommends that the technical and economic staff of the Bank should be increased to give advice even where a loan is not sought and to draw up new projects and endeavor to interest private companies in executing them. In such instances, equity participation by the Bank may be necessary.

Possible Industrial Projects

The 1961 Mission listed some industrial possibilities which should be investigated. As all are being considered, but apparently no definite decision has been reached on the majority, the list is reproduced below.

Glass Factory. Several searches have been made to discover suitable sands for glass manufacture. Although possibilities can by no means be considered exhausted, present indications are that there are deposits of sand suitable for bottles but not white enough for window glass. The demand for soft-drink bottles is about 2 million per year. At present, bottles are brought from Western Europe, and freight is very high. Manufacture of 2 million bottles would be commercially attractive for a glass factory, especially as fuel (natural gas) would be cheap and soda would be the only imported material. In this field, where freight and breakage rates are high, exports of bottles to neighboring countries should be possible.

Tire Factory. Sales of tires in Kuwait probably amount to over 100,000 per year. This may not be large enough to support a tire factory to compete with imported tires. It is, however, large enough to support a factory for remoulds. There are several plants for retreading tires by recapping or remoulding. In a hot climate there is a grave danger of the treads being thrown off, if process control such as is only possible in a factory is not rigidly enforced. Remoulding under controlled conditions, however, is very successful, and it would be possible to produce reconditioned tires for less than half the cost of imports of new tires. It should be possible to capture about half the market.

Paint. Paint deteriorates seriously if it is left in stock longer than one year. It is very difficult to forecast sales by paint type and by color, and this tends to increase stock levels and the length of time paint has to be kept. The usual solution to this problem is to import the ingredients and mix the paints as required. A small paint factory run on these lines would be very practicable.

Batteries. Car batteries have a short life in the hot climate, and last only about one year. This gives a possible market of about 40,000 batteries per year. Provided prices are substantially below those of known makes, local batteries should take at least half the market. The process would have to be decided from detailed costing, but taking into consideration the size of the market and the shortage of skilled operators, only an assembly operation would seem practicable. That is, plates, boxes and bitumen would be imported by agreement with a foreign manufacturer and the battery assembled and filled with acid in Kuwait.

Slaughterhouse By-Products. Plans are in hand to build a municipal slaughterhouse. This will handle about 1,000 animals a day, and could form a basis for a small industry to use all the by-products. For instance, the blood can be dried for use as a fertilizer, the bones may be boiled and fats extracted for use in soap and glue-making, while the rendered bones make an excellent fertilizer or can be made into cattle feed.

Flour Mill and Cattle and Chicken Feed Plant. A flour mill is being constructed in the dock area. Imports of flour are about 40,000 tons per year, and this is large enough to establish a medium-sized, modern mill. It would be highly advantageous if this could be integrated with a plant producing chicken and cattle food, as these can be made partly of by-products from a flour mill. If a fishmeal factory is also established, its output can be used in this plant.

Chemicals. Small amounts of salt, soda and other chemicals will undoubtedly be produced if a chemical complex is established based on natural gas. These would satisfy home demand, but would not command export markets. Considerable economies can be made in buying the more common pharmaceuticals such as aspirin, ingredients for health salts, and the like in bulk, and tableting and packaging them in a laboratory-type factory. This would be an inexpensive plant to erect and, provided the products are packaged well and marketed correctly, the enterprise could be profitable.

Furniture. A good deal of furniture is made in Kuwait, most of it for institutional use and government housing. Government departments are making an effort to raise the quality by inviting international tender and by producing demonstration samples at the required standard. Speed and expediency, however, often force acceptance of home-produced furniture of a lower standard.

Low quality is not essentially caused by poor raw materials used, lack of skill on the part of the workmen or even the desire of management to boost profits. It is lack of discrimination and experience on the part of management in identifying the attributes of high-quality production. However, when modern furniture machinery is installed, local factories could certainly satisfy a good portion of the rather sizable home market and stand some chance in exports.

Radios and Electrical Appliances. Although radios and electrical appliances generally have to be mass-produced to be economical, some assembly work could be carried out locally. It would be practicable to import radio and later television chassis, and to make cabinets which are suitably designed for the domestic market.

Steel. If a direct (sponge) iron plant is to be installed after appropriate testing of the ore to be used, a small steel plant could use a combination of local scrap and direct iron. Scrap produced is stated to be some 100,000 tons per year. However, even if it is as high as this, not all would be usable locally. The most practicable policy would be to establish a rerolling mill first, to produce reinforcing iron from scrap-rolled sections. Later, a small steel plant to melt the scrap and roll to shape could be installed.

Food Factories. Some biscuits, candies and cakes are produced at home and sold in the streets. Eventually there will be a desire to have these produced more hygienically, and then small factories can be started. If a vegetable-growing industry is started, seasonal surpluses are inevitable. The excess vegetables can be canned. This will, of course, only pay if surplus and therefore cheap vegetables are used.

Building and Construction Materials. Although there will be a continuing demand for building materials, the Mission feels that this industry has already been overdone and that, in general, further installations to supply building materials should be discouraged.[7]

---

[7] Many steel windows are produced locally, and the quality is extremely low compared with the imported windows. Lack of experience results in buying poor quality window sections, but the main reason is the primitive production methods employed. For instance, in a typical shop the bars were first straightened with a hammer and then cut to length with an emery wheel; the corners were welded and the frames assembled without fitting.

The initial straightening operation should not be necessary with good-quality bars and, in any case, it ruins the section. Bars should be clipped to length in a

However, suitable deposits of limestone and clay have been located, as previously mentioned, and the National Industries Company has decided to build a plant for making Portland cement. This can probably be a success.

Other Private Sector Productive Activities

Fishing. The development of fishing seems to be a sound proposition. Admittedly, no adequate investigation has yet been undertaken of the total fishing potential of the Gulf. But the intensity of fishing is low, and the risk of "fishing out" the Gulf seems to be small if appropriate rules on minimum net meshes are applied to avoid destroying young fish.

The owners of the present Gulf Fisheries Company described in Chapter 4 have studied the possibility of extending the industry, building a factory in order to produce canned fish, fish meal and other products. This would include an extension of the fleet. In order to be able to fish a greater part of the year, catches of fish for consumption would be increased, too, partly for export to some of the neighboring countries; in order to support a development of large-scale fishing, it is important to allow free and unconditional export of all types of fish, even those usually consumed in Kuwait. The factories would be built either in Kuwait or in Dubai.[8]

It is in the interests of Kuwait that this development take place. Admittedly, it might create difficulties for the small amount of fishing

---

press which is quicker and does not leave a snag to be removed. Corners should be flash butt-welded to avoid distortion, and the small flash should be cleaned by a press rather than by grinding. After the frames are put together, they should be adjusted to ensure that both faces of the section match. The windows should be galvanized; but if they are not, at least the rust should be removed chemically and a paint primer should be put on.

This description has been given in some detail to illustrate how the quality can be transformed by minor alterations in equipment and work organization.

[8] A specific problem arises concerning the site of the factory for processing the fish. The western end of the new harbor in Shuwaikh has been proposed, but the capacity of the new harbor is nearly completely used, and space for future port expansion might be needed. In addition, the factory might give rise to unpleasant smells, even if modern methods of production are adopted. A site south of Mina Al Ahmadi in connection with the new development of heavy industry therefore might be preferred. Fish could be graded on the trawlers, fresh fish boxed and landed in the City, while the rest would be landed at the factory and canned or made into fish meal.

being done by the old-fashioned methods, not because the sea would be "fished out," but because large-scale fishing probably would mean lower prices of fish in Kuwait and make traditional fishing even less profitable than it is today. It is questionable, however, whether it is desirable—or even possible—to give sufficient protection to preserve this old style of fishing.

Agriculture. Green vegetables, imported by truck from Lebanon, Syria or Jordan, are several days on the road and arrive in poor condition. While the possibility of reducing transportation costs should be considered, it also would be advantageous if some of these vegetables could be grown in Kuwait at competitive prices. Green vegetables have been grown by the Experimental Farm on a scale large enough to show that this is practicable.

Consumption of fresh vegetables amounts to some 11,000 tons per year. Yields per hectare of vegetables grown on a commercial scale are not known, but from results obtained on the Experimental Farm it would appear that this tonnage could be produced on 300–400 hectares, and that it could be economically feasible to grow certain types of vegetables. Means of obtaining an adequate water supply are discussed in Chapter 7.[9]

Neither the demand for fresh milk nor the yield from cattle fed on alfalfa in Kuwait is accurately known. It does appear, however, that 300 hectares planted with alfalfa, which at present is grown with brackish water, would provide food for enough cattle to supply about 25 per cent of the present market for dairy products. Dairy herds are feasible for the sake of fresh milk, but keeping fat stock would not be economic. It should be possible, however, to feed imported livestock long enough to improve their condition before slaughter.

[9] The 1961 Mission made the following calculations:
It costs KD 150 per 10-ton truck to bring vegetables overland from Lebanon. If we assume that, except for water, the costs of producing vegetables in Kuwait are the same as in Lebanon, we might arrive at a maximum permissible cost of water by equating such cost to that for transportation of vegetables from Lebanon to Kuwait. Assuming transport is by truck, the water could be priced at 150 fils per 1,000 gallons. Such vegetables as tomatoes and lettuce, however, arrive in a poor condition if brought by truck, and considerable quantities are flown in. This costs approximately 25 fils per pound, and so the producer could afford to pay 500 fils per 1,000 gallons for irrigation water. As noted below, brackish water is now sold for 150 fils per 1,000 gallons. Thus, Kuwait could probably grow vegetables on a competitive basis if the cost of water were reduced as suggested in Chapter 7. Of course, commercial production might give rise to technical problems which should be carefully studied as the enterprise develops.

It is not expected that production of grain crops will ever be economical in Kuwait. A balanced meal for poultry can, however, be made with imported grain, extended with locally produced fish meal and chopped leguminous crops. If a flour mill is erected, a by-product will be bran, and this can be used to provide bulk in poultry meal.

Shipping. There is a world surplus of ships in general and of oil tankers in particular. In the latter category, however, the oil companies would probably agree to use Kuwait tankers rather than an independent charter company, provided rates are competitive. The Kuwait Tanker Company's single vessel is operated on this basis.

The size of tankers has increased greatly during the last five years, and the smaller tankers tend to be laid up. The average dead weight tonnage of the world's tanker fleet is 19,000 tons, while the average weight of those laid up is 14,000 tons. The boats laid up represent 5 per cent of the world's carrying capacity, while those being built will add another 26 per cent.

General indications are that although world trade in oil will increase, seaborne oil will not increase very much over the next three or four years. These facts indicate that world freight rates will remain low. On the other hand, a 46,000-ton tanker can be run more cheaply than a 16,000-ton ship per ton of oil. Taking depreciation and interest at 10 per cent for the large tanker, and even assuming the small one is already written off, costs per ton of oil are just about equal.

The indications are that a few new large tankers built by Kuwait could pay their way, and might very well make profits if the enterprise were well managed. This is a field in which Kuwaiti traditional talents can be applied.

CHAPTER 9 *PUBLIC HEALTH*
AND SOCIAL WELFARE

PUBLIC HEALTH

The first health service in Kuwait was established in 1910, when Sheikh Mubarak invited the Dutch Reformed Church of America to extend its work to his country. In 1911 it established the first clinic, and in 1912 a hospital was started. The Mission Hospital and a free dispensary under the British Political Agency Medical Officer were the only medical facilities until the middle of the 1940s when the first government clinics were established.

Since 1949, Kuwait public medical services have developed at a rapid pace. Today there is a full-fledged health ministry. All residents are registered with clinics which provide "family doctor" type services and which maintain the individual medical files. Polyclinics—one to each three or four clinics—provide 24-hour emergency service and special service such as dental treatment. Medical services are free to residents of Kuwait and to visitors alike. No one goes without medical care if he applies for it. The health services are comparable in quality to those in developed countries. Some special problems exist, however, in the preventive aspect of health activities and in over-all public health administration.

The Public Health Ministry is responsible for all curative and preventive health services in Kuwait. Under the Minister and Under Secretary, the technical aspects of the activities are the responsibility of a chief medical officer who is assisted by a deputy chief medical officer. All the services are integrated at this level.

Preventive Health Services Section

This section bears the responsibility for protecting the population of Kuwait against disease, and endeavors to promote the standard of health as a whole. In spite of its important responsibilities, it is not as yet equipped with sufficient personnel and physical facilities.

The Service is responsible for general communicable diseases control and environmental sanitation. It is not responsible for tuberculosis and venereal disease control, which are dealt with by independent services. It maintains health offices around the country, each supposed to consist of one physician, one sanitary inspector, two sanitary aides and a nurse. However, at present a total of only six physicians is available for this work.

The General Public Health Laboratory is annexed to the Amiri Hospital. Due to overload of work, however, small laboratories have been developed and there is a tendency to expand them. The Preventive Medicine Division has a laboratory meant for public health activities, but for lack of facilities, its work today is restricted to the examination of food handlers and to food analysis.

School Health Service

This Service is responsible for the health of school children, of the teaching staff and of auxiliary personnel working in teaching institutions. There are about 127 schools, and each school has a clinic, with a physician for approximately every five schools. In addition to the school clinics, there is a central clinic where specialized treatment is given. This includes a skin and venereal diseases section, an ophthalmological section, an ear, nose and throat section and a dental section. A small laboratory and a pharmacy are also available. A recent addition is a chest clinic with specialists, nurses, X-ray units and clerks working as a team to examine school children by doing mass X-ray, tuberculine tests, and vaccination.

A general physical examination is given to all newcomers in each school at the beginning of each scholastic year. In addition, a more routine examination is made of all school children. Vaccination is done regularly against smallpox, whooping cough, and diphtheria, and is now a compulsory prerequisite to school registration. Several special surveys and campaigns have been carried out recently against tuberculosis, trachoma, dental cavities, skin diseases and congenital defects.

School sanitation is supervised by two health inspectors who visit the schools periodically. Water samples are collected and analyzed every month. This section also deals with the sanitary condition of school buildings.

The School Health Service also promotes health education. In each school there is a health society with the objective of propagating health habits and health interests.

An outstanding and unusual feature of the school system is the Central Kitchen. It prepares food for about 50,000 school children, teachers and auxiliary personnel of the schools. At least one meal a day is given to everybody. A certain number get two meals, and a smaller group gets three meals. The meals are prepared with due consideration to calories and food value. The kitchen is under the Ministry of Education, but its health aspects are an additional responsibility of the School Health Service.

Social Health Centers

The main concern of this Service is the protection of mothers and of children up to the age of 12. Emphasis is placed on the curative side. The work started in 1956 with the institution of four centers which have now been increased to seven or eight. The workload of these centers is quite heavy, especially as regards children's examinations and treatment. Home visiting is restricted to a minimum. The 1961 Mission estimated that an average of 180 children were examined daily in some of the centers.

The number of child deliveries assisted by the service reached nearly 4,000 in 1960, an increase of 73 per cent since 1956. This number represents about 34 per cent of the births in Kuwait. In 1961, it was estimated that about 50 per cent of the deliveries attended were performed in hospitals.

Vaccinations are performed against smallpox, diphtheria, pertussis (whooping cough), tetanus and, to a small extent, poliomyelitis. A clinic for family planning is also run by this Service.

Quarantine Division

This Division is responsible for the control of all passengers entering by air, land and sea. The Division comprises quarantine stations in Kuwait airport, Kuwait port, Mina Al Ahmadi and nine lesser centers. In four quarantine stations, out-patient clinics operate for passengers and seafarers. Insect and rodent control in port areas also is undertaken by this Division.

Health Education Division

This Division was established in 1960. It was previously part of the Preventive Medicine Division. Its activities are numerous. A monthly magazine is issued called "The Community Physician" addressed to the general public. Radio programs are given twice a week on health problems and attitudes. Pamphlets, posters and films are used regularly. Further plans are under study to expand health education by including more items in the training courses for health personnel, by appropriate approaches during treatment of patients in clinics and by appeals in public gathering places. The importance of health education is recognized by the health services of Kuwait, and every effort is being made to perform and further expand the important and basic task of disseminating health knowledge, indoctrinating the people with a consciousness of health problems and promoting higher health standards.

Curative Medicine Activities

The Health Ministry's principal activities dealing with curative medicine are as follows:

Out-Patient Clinics Division. There are more than 30 out-patient clinics, chiefly concerned with general curative activities. For any specialized examination or treatment, patients are usually referred to hospitals. Laboratory examinations are referred to the central laboratory in the Amiri Hospital.

In the clinics run by the Public Health Department, there is a system of registration. However, this does not eliminate multiple use of parallel available services, and duplication is often experienced. It is estimated that in 1960, ten calls per capita were made at all clinics of the Health Department, not including dental services. In the Mission's opinion this number of calls was excessive.

Hospital Facilities. Kuwait has developed full-scale hospital services which are provided free to all inhabitants. In Table 16, present hospital facilities are given. The number of admissions to hospitals in 1960 was 24,294, so that about 8 per cent of the population was being admitted to the hospitals per year. In addition, the number of patients attending the out-patient clinics in the general hospitals was 484,358 and for the sanatoria and Mental Hospital, 102,113 and 8,120, respectively.

TABLE 16

Type of Hospital	Number of Beds
General Hospitals	1,147
Maternity	252
Orthopedic	189
T. B. Sanitarium and Preventorium	964
Mental Hospital	280
Typhus (fever)	85
Leprosarium	21
Radiotherapy	20
Total	2,958

Table 17 gives some comparative data in respect to hospital
facilities as between Kuwait and other countries. In appraising these
figures, it should be kept in mind that they do not provide entirely
comparable data in view of differences in definitions of hospitals
and personnel which vary from country to country, differences in the
incidence of diseases and other factors.

TABLE 17

	Kuwait	Canada	U.K.	Sweden	U.S.
Hospital Beds per 1,000					
Population [a]	8.4[b]	11.6	10.8	15.0	9.2
of which:					
Tuberculosis	2.8	0.98	0.57	1.05	0.5
Maternity	0.7		0.44	0.33	0.5
Mental	0.8	4.2	3.5	4.4	3.9

[a] Data for Canada, U.K., Sweden and U.S. in 1957.
[b] The population of Kuwait is estimated at 350,000 for purposes of this table.

Non-Government Health Services

KOC. The Kuwait Oil Company runs a public health service in
Ahmadi and a hospital mainly for company personnel and their
families. Service includes communicable diseases control, maternal
and child health activities, vaccinations, school health, veterinary
services and general sanitation. There are four out-patient clinics,
three of which are run outside Ahmadi, where the Company has
additional installations. In 1961 hospital facilities comprised 200
beds for general purposes.

Dutch Reformed Church Mission Hospital. This Mission, the first to
introduce modern medicine to Kuwait, runs a hospital and an out-
patient clinic which comprises almost every specialized field. In 1961
the personnel in the hospital and out-patient clinics consisted of 9
physicians and 32 qualified and non-qualified nurses. The Mission
Hospital charges its patients for its services; but free care is given to
the destitute.

Health Statistics

Generally speaking, vital and health statistics collected in Kuwait
are inadequate and probably misleading. According to data collected
by the 1961 Mission, the birth rates are estimated to have been 25,
29.7 and 35.4 per 1,000, respectively, for 1958, 1959 and 1960. Reported

death rates for the same years were 3.2, 3.4 and 4.1 per 1,000, respectively. These data, while probably not reliable, reflected the very unusual age distribution of the population. Only about 2.2 per cent were over 65.

The main registered causes of death are heart diseases, enteritis and colitis, diseases of the respiratory system, diseases of early infancy, congenital malformation and turberculosis. The most prevalent diseases are chickenpox, tuberculosis, measles, bacillary and amoebic dysentery and whooping cough. Infant mortality per 1,000 was estimated at 17.1, 14.5 and 23.8 in 1958, 1959 and 1960, respectively. The data probably understate the true rates because of deficiency in registration. It seems likely that most deaths registered are among the more settled and well-to-do members of the population, though they may include a substantial number of visitors who died in hospital. The higher infant mortality rate for 1960 probably reflects improved coverage of registration rather than a high rate of mortality.

Health Personnel and Their Training

Health personnel are in great majority non-Kuwaitis. There were only four Kuwaiti physicians in 1961, three of whom were in the Health Department. No qualified nurses or qualified health inspectors were of Kuwaiti nationality. This situation may have changed somewhat, though most Kuwaitis going into medicine are still studying abroad.

The following tabulation gives the number of physicians and nursing personnel in Kuwait in 1961 as compared with other countries. The figures concerning Kuwait do not include the personnel of the KOC. In appraising these figures, it should be noted that differences exist between one country and another in definitions of doctors and nurses and in the level of professional and academic training.

TABLE 18 [a]

	Kuwait	Canada	U.K.	Sweden	U.S.
Number of Inhabitants per Physician [b]	1,069	950	900	1,200	790
Number of Inhabitants per Nurse [c]	251	191	—	130	340

[a] Data for countries other than Kuwait, from Annual Epidemiological and Vital Statistics, 1957; WHO, 1960.

[b] Data for Canada and Sweden in 1957, for U.K. and U.S. in 1958. Kuwait is based on 1961 tentative census results.

[c] Data for U.S. in 1956, for Canada, U.K., and Sweden in 1957.

Training facilities for health personnel consist mainly of in-service training. An informal training course for sanitary inspectors has been developed, however, and is run by personnel of the Public Health Department. This is a nine-month course, and the students are mainly from personnel in the service. An attempt to develop a training course for nurses has been made but was not successful due to lack of students. There is also a course for midwives of three years' duration but the difficulty of recruiting students is encountered here, too.

Eighty-six students in medicine and dentistry were studying abroad on scholarships in 1963/64. In addition, 22 students were training abroad to become medical technicians. This is an increase of about one-third over the past two or three years in the number of students pursuing foreign studies related to public health.

Current Public Health Problems

Town and Village Sanitation. The strenuous climatic conditions and the physical bleakness of the desert are being countered by an unprecedented and spectacular effort to bring about a transformation in a relatively short time. This unique undertaking could not but engender great problems in the field of environmental sanitation. Such problems are made greater and their scope broader because of the disparity between previous conditions and present aspirations. Deficiencies in the field of environmental sanitation in old Kuwait might have been of only secondary importance, but today any weakness would bring about a potential threat to health and well-being. A balanced development cannot be envisaged without giving to environmental sanitation problems the thought, study and solution they require. They represent the most pressing problems in the field of health.

Several ministries are now concerned with sanitation. Garbage collection, transfer and disposal are all responsibilities of the Municipality, together with the various inspection services noted above; but the Municipality relies on Ministry of Health personnel for help in these matters, and the Ministry is responsible for fly and rodent control, which is closely related to the Municipality's activities. And while the Ministry of Power and Water is, of course, responsible for the production and distribution of water, the sampling of water for health protection is a function of Public Health Services. Some coordinating body on which these various agencies would be represented is desirable.

Water Supply—Health Aspects. The production and distribution of water supply were described in Chapter 4 of this report. The City of Kuwait has a dual-water system, one providing brackish and the other potable water. The brackish water is piped to the user in some cases, whereas the potable water is almost all delivered by truck.

The present system of distributing potable water by tanks and trucks cannot be considered free from danger on public health grounds. The Preventive Medicine Section of Public Health samples the water periodically and carries out bacteriological analyses which seem to be satisfactory. It is advisable to extend the sampling, however, and it would be useful to introduce the WHO standards for drinking water.

A proposal exists for developing a complete pipe distribution network for the brackish water. This water is meant for cleaning purposes and irrigation; it might be dangerous to health if piped into bathrooms and other outlets alongside fresh water without proper safeguards. Its easy availability and its comparatively low price might induce its use as potable and domestic water. The present installations do not guarantee its bacteriological quality; and the relatively high content of fluorine (3.5 parts per million) is a matter which requires closer study (cases of fluorosis in skeletons have been recorded among Arabs in the Gulf area). The development of a potable water supply network should have priority over the proposed extension of the brackish water distribution system, and should be provided first.

The danger that a dual-water supply involves is well known, and sad experiences have been registered. Such a supply can be acceptable, however, if properly applied, as in Ahmadi, where there is a full distribution net with individual house connections for every consumer for brackish as well as potable water. It should preclude any accidental mixture with brackish water, and should discourage or prevent, where possible, the use of brackish water for domestic purposes where only potable water should be used.

The potable water coming from the mixture of the distillage and a small percentage of brackish water is chlorinated with two parts per million chlorine. In spite of this chlorination, little or no chlorine is found in various parts of the distribution system. This requires an investigation.

Such pipes as exist for distributing fresh water are mainly cast iron. Much trouble is experienced from corrosion, probably together with growth of iron and sulphur bacteria, and the resulting formation of "red water." Recently, asbestos pipes have begun to be introduced. It may be appropriate to investigate the possibility of chemical treatment of the water at the distillation plant to reduce corrosion until asbestos pipes will take care of this problem entirely.

Refuse Disposal. As already mentioned, in Kuwait City the collection and disposal of refuse is the responsibility of the Municipality. At present, refuse is simply dumped in an open area outside town. No sanitary handling of these wastes is provided, and the breeding of flies and other related nuisances is abundant. The treatment and adequate disposal of the refuse as well as the possibility of producing a needed fertilizer is under study. Several methods and offers are under consideration for the treatment of the crude refuse and also for the application of composting in conjunction with sludge disposal. In this connection it appears to be useful to consider also the sanitary landfill method which, noting the conditions in Kuwait, seems to be most promising and relatively cheap. This latter system is being used in Ahmadi town and is giving satisfactory results.

Other Sanitary Problems. Under construction in Kuwait are various market places for fish, meat and vegetables which will greatly improve the hygienic marketing conditions of food. Conditions of meat and food hygiene outside Kuwait City and Ahmadi leave room for great improvement.

There is no industrial health service or industrial hygiene control in the public services of Kuwait. With the development of the country and the proposed increase of industrial activities, it seems necessary that some steps be taken toward the development of an appropriate service. Some health problems connected with industry and with labor forces already exist, and the need for proper handling and control will soon become pressing. The Ministry of Social Affairs deals with labor, but apparently its work is limited to the application of existing laws regarding employment. It does not deal with industrial medicine or industrial hygiene.

Housing. Outside the town of Kuwait there are four relatively extended areas where people live under slum conditions. The number living in these slums could not be ascertained except for Ashairig, which has about 12,000 people, but the total is estimated to be relatively high. In addition to the slum areas, there is poor housing in villages which needs rehabilitation. The development of an adequate neighborhood also comes into the picture; it constitutes the necessary frame and supplement for providing healthy housing.

Housing conditions represent a definite problem not only for the areas where they prevail but also for Kuwait City itself. The extreme difference between the city life and that in the nearby slum areas or in the villages can only influence the development of Kuwait City unfavorably.

Immigration Supervision. A large part of immigration into Kuwait is from the diseased portion of the populations of the neighboring countries in the region. While the free medical services furnished by Kuwait to all those in the State are very praiseworthy, the large number of transients and other relatively uncontrolled movements of the population put a great burden on the Preventive Medicine Section of the Ministry and, more important, represent a considerable health hazard. The recent registration of the expatriate labor force indicated that about a third had entered illegally without a check of any kind. More adequate migration controls are necessary in addition to the efforts already made in this direction.

Safety in Industry. There are some regulations about working hours and safety in factories, but the Department of Social Affairs has not yet been able to enforce them. The members of the Mission saw many examples of factory practice which are extremely undesirable and dangerous. Examples are unguarded machinery and belts, passages immediately behind saw operators, unshielded electric arcs, machine operators with loose clothing.

Owners and managers will, no doubt, resent interference in the running of their plants. It is therefore important to employ factory inspectors who are practical and positive in their approach. That is, they should help owners to make their factories safe, and not simply look for legal contraventions. Nevertheless, in cases of non-cooperation, they should be empowered to prosecute.

The work of these inspectors will cover many fields, including health, safety and working hours. To have several government departments inspecting a factory would result in resentment and lack of cooperation. It is therefore recommended that one section only should be formed. As health regulations have the broadest application, it would be most appropriate to have the inspectors responsible to Public Health. Of course other ministries would promulgate regulations, and would have power to request information and returns from the inspectors.

Research in Public Health

Kuwait should develop research activities in public health, and should install services not possible in other countries of the area. The installation of a cobalt bomb for cancer control and research is an example; but many more could be added, particularly research on diseases of the eyes and other ailments common to arid countries. Public Health officials suggested the following research projects which seem to have merit: (1) insect classification, determination of their breeding and feeding habits, resting places, resistance to insecticides and other biological factors; (2) rodent-pesticide research on the same line; and (3) the investigation of certain communicable diseases in the area, especially the virus and rickettsial diseases.

Capital Expenditures on Health

The principal capital expenditures contemplated for public health facilities during the next three years are a new 600-bed general hospital (Mubarak), annexes to the mental and chest diseases hospitals, a medical warehouse, and additional facilities for the Sanatorium and the Al Sabah Hospital. These plans will require over KD 8 million, and seem to cover adequately the needs of Kuwait for the present and near future. The aim of the Ministry is to provide about 10 hospital beds per 1,000 inhabitants as compared with 8.4 at present. Some additional capital expenditures for research facilities would seem to be justified.

SOCIAL WELFARE

In addition to its program in education and health, Kuwait has made fairly comprehensive provision for public assistance in various forms. It also has a minimum wage law for government workers and regulations affecting employment in the private section.

The minimum wage for government workers is the equivalent of $1.89 per day (675 fils), and this tends to establish a minimum for private employment as well. The minimum age for employment in the private sector is 12 years, and persons between the age of 12 and 17 years may not be employed without authorization from the Ministry of Social Affairs. Women may not be employed in dangerous occupations or on night shifts, and are entitled to equal pay for equal work. Except under special circumstances, the maximum work week is 48 hours in private industry. Employees whose job is terminated are entitled to 15 days of pay for each of the first five years of service and one month's pay for each subsequent year. Employers are required to pay all expenses incident to injuries or disease sustained as a result of employment.

The Public Assistance Law was passed in 1962. It attempts to provide help to individuals and families who have met with misfortune, and to restore them to productive employment after their immediate needs have been met. Widows, orphans, disabled and diseased persons, the aged, and very low-income families are the principal categories to which the law applies. The Ministry of Social Affairs provides assistance ranging from KD 11.25 to a maximum of KD 30 per month, plus a housing allowance for those requiring it. In the calendar year 1962, 3,388 persons were helped under the Public Assistance Law.

An interesting feature of the Kuwait social welfare system are the measures taken to assist persons to establish themselves in business. For example, financial assistance covering a whole year may be given in a lump sum if it seems that the recipient can utilize this capital productively. Also, the Ministry is given broad discretion in justifying ways of training or otherwise rehabilitating recipients of assistance. Since 1956, the Ministry has been carrying out the so-called "kiosk scheme." The recipient is supplied with a small shop (kiosk), a refrigerator and some goods for retailing to the public. This scheme, open only to Kuwaiti nationals, apparently has been quite successful in restoring indigents to a self-supporting basis. In 1956, the Ministry of Social Affairs established a girls' training institute to provide vocational training to Kuwaiti girls who had missed it when they were younger. The institute has a fairly broad curriculum, including social and commercial studies. The Government has also established welfare institutions for old and disabled persons, and children.

Thus, while Kuwait lacks an organized system of old-age pensions or unemployment insurance, its social welfare program is quite broad and humanitarian. Since the affluence of Kuwait leads many organizations from other Arab communities to try to solicit assistance in the State, the Government has found it necessary to screen these organizations and try to assure the proper use of private benefactions. During 1961, about half the 54 applicant organizations were permitted to try to collect funds from the private sector by the Ministry of Social Affairs.

CHAPTER 10 *EDUCATION*

During the last decade, the educational changes that have occurred in Kuwait have perhaps been more pronounced than in any other field. The Government's interest in education is very keen and the Ministry of Education has wisely sought advice from abroad.

In 1952, two Egyptian scholars were invited to study the educational system. Their main task was to suggest curricula changes to secure the endorsement of the Kuwaiti secondary school graduates for study in higher institutions in Egypt. Another, much more comprehensive, study of education was undertaken in 1955 by Ismail Al Qabbani, a former Minister of Education in Egypt, and Dr. Matta Akrawi, the former President of Baghdad University. Most of the educational changes which took place in Kuwait after 1955 were influenced by their proposals which included the present ladder of education, a revision of the school curricula, a comprehensive program of adult education and the opening of teachers' colleges.

In 1960, Sir Ivor Jennings, Dr. Suleiman Huzain and Dr. Constantin Zureiq were invited to investigate the possibility of establishing a university in Kuwait. This University Advisory Commission recommended that a university be established. The Kuwait Government has accepted the Commission's proposals in principle, though the matter is still under consideration.

Summary of Present System

Educational Ladder. The ladder of education is in three stages, each of four years: the primary, the intermediate and the secondary. The 12 years of this ladder are preceded by the kindergarten, which accepts children between four and six. Separate but about equal educational facilities are provided for both sexes.

The emphasis in the primary and intermediate schools is on the mastery of reading, writing and arithmetic, and on the mental and physical development of the children. A public examination is held by the Ministry at the end of the four-year intermediate course. Students who pass this examination are entitled to enter the secondary schools.

Secondary education is of two types, academic and vocational. It qualifies students for admission to higher institutions in the Arab countries of the Middle East, particularly Egypt, and, with certain

144

reservations, to the universities in the United Kingdom and the United States. The first two years of the secondary school are of a general nature, whereas in the last two years the students follow either a literary or a scientific course. Vocational secondary education is also of two types, technical and commercial.

There is one commercial school, held in the evening, in which two different courses are provided. One course follows the pattern of the ordinary secondary school, i.e., a four-year course after intermediate education. The other is for government and private employees. This course is of two years' duration and the emphasis is on typing—Arabic and English—accounting, secretarial work, office management, plus general background courses in Arabic and English. The ability to read and write seems to be the only condition for admission.

The Technical College, the only technical school in Kuwait, was established in 1954. At that time, graduates of the primary school were admitted, with carpentry as the only course. Now, however, the Technical College provides a four-year course, along the lines of the technical school program in Egypt. The student may specialize in any one of 12 branches such as electricity, auto mechanics, carpentry and building construction. There are also teacher training schools for men and women which students holding the intermediate school certificate may attend.

The material incentives utilized in encouraging enrollment at the teacher training schools and the Technical College proved to be very successful. For example, in 1963/64 there were 384 students at the Technical College as compared with only 185 in 1960/61, and 400 girls at the Women's Teacher Training School as compared with only 76 in the earlier year.

Along with the regular ladder of education there are the following schools: Al-Mahad Al-Dini, a religious institution, where the syllabus in the primary school is the same as that of the ordinary primary school but differs slightly in the intermediate and still more in the secondary level. Here Arabic, the Koran and the Islamic law and institutions are emphasized. Graduates are admitted to Al-Azhar University in Cairo. Second, there is a large institution which comprises three schools, for the blind, for the deaf and for the mentally retarded children.

While education in Kuwait is essentially a government responsibility, there are 18 private schools, notably the Anglo-American and the India-Pakistani schools in Ahmadi which are run by KOC. The Ministry of Education supervises the private schools.

Kuwait has recognized the importance of adult education. Although as yet there is no comprehensive program in this field, a good start has been made. The Ministry of Social Affairs, in cooperation with other ministries, especially Education, conducts centers for combating illiteracy—all for men.

Students in Kuwait are exceptionally well provided for. All tuition is, of course, gratis, as are books and other school supplies. The health facilities and free meals were mentioned in the previous chapter. At the Technical College, students receive free board and lodging and a monthly allowance, and at the teacher training schools, they receive free clothing as well.

Sending students abroad for study began almost from the time modern education took shape in Kuwait. Until 1950, the majority of the Kuwaitis who were sent abroad for study were in secondary school. But in 1960/61, 470 students received scholarships for higher education abroad, and in 1963/64, 543. Scholarship students study mainly in the United Arab Republic, the United Kingdom and the United States. The breakdown by lines of study of the students now abroad is given in Statistical Annex Table XV. Not much change in fields of specialization has occurred since 1961.

Since 1952, Kuwait has established a number of schools outside Kuwait. By 1961, there were 16 such schools in the Gulf Sheikhdoms—primary, intermediate and secondary—with a student enrollment of 3,886. Teachers' salaries, books, stationery, food and medical services and all other expenses are borne by Kuwait. Kuwait also provides scholarships for students from the Gulf Sheikhdoms to study abroad. In addition, there were 174 students from the Arab world studying in Kuwait at the expense of the Government.

Growth in Student Numbers. The growth in the school population is shown in Table 19.

TABLE 19

	Number of Students			Proportion of:	
Academic Year	Boys	Girls	Total	Boys (%)	Girls (%)
1936/37	600	0	600	100.00	0
1946/47	3,037	935	3,962	76.60	23.59
1956/57	15,946	8,578	24,524	65.02	34.97
1960/61	27,698	17,459	45,157	61.33	38.67
1962/63	35,674	23,877	59,551	49.91	40.09

In 1956/57, there were 119 students per 1,000 of the population.[1] This ratio undoubtedly was the highest so far achieved by any Arab state. Now there are about 170 per 1,000. Between the academic years 1962/63 and 1963/64, the number of students increased by 19 per cent and number of classes by 15 per cent (see Statistical Annex Table XVI). There was a rather sharp drop in students enrolled in vocational schools but a much greater increase in secondary and special school enrollments.

The education of girls started somewhat later than that of boys. In 1936 there were no girls in Kuwait schools. At the present time, however, the number of girls in the kindergarten and in the primary schools is almost on a par with that of the boys. There is every reason to believe that equality will be achieved in the intermediate schools during the coming few years.

Teachers. In the academic year 1963/64, there were 3,575 teachers employed in Kuwait. The student-teacher ratio seems quite good, 21.6 for the primary and intermediate, 13.6 for the secondary, and 6.5 for vocational and special schools. It is interesting that nearly half (47%) of the teachers are women. However, 95 per cent are expatriates. About 30 per cent of the teachers are college graduates, which may be considered rather low. Only about 53 per cent have had professional training in education.

Buildings and Equipment. Most of the school buildings are magnificent in construction, size, equipment and other facilities. They compare favorably with the best modern schools anywhere. In fact, perhaps simpler and more functional structures would serve better, or at least as well.

Goals of Education in Kuwait

Kuwait, at this stage of its development, is faced with problems of adjustment to rapid change. The discrepancy between the old Arab way of life and modern civilization, and the speed with which the old ways are being challenged, are at the heart of these problems. Sound education combats stagnation. It must also take into account that Kuwait is an Arab and Moslem country. The Mission believes that with eight years of compulsory education it is possible to provide the new generation with the needed tools and understandings.

---

[1] Accepting the 1957 census as valid. In view of the 1961 census, the 1957 census results would seem to err on the low side, and the student-to-population ratio may have been lower than here stated.

Along with this compulsory education for the young, Kuwait needs a comprehensive program in adult education.

To summarize, we believe that the educational system of Kuwait should strive to:

a) equip the younger generation with the knowledge, skills, habits, and attitudes needed in a changing society;

b) create a respect for mental and manual work and provide sound vocational as well as academic training;

c) cultivate a sense of national respect among the Kuwaitis;

d) stimulate their appreciation of democracy as a way of life;

e) cultivate originality in art, music, and other cultural fields; and

f) make a contribution to the education of the region.

To achieve these goals is not an easy job. It needs the cooperation of the Government and the people. The great variety of nationalities and cultural backgrounds among the people add to the problem.

School Curricula

In general, Kuwait, especially at the secondary school level, is following a curriculum similar to that of Egypt. Principles of educational growth and basic needs of children are the same all over the world; but conditions of life and income in Kuwait are different from those in Egypt. The curriculum in the Kuwait schools, therefore, should be constructed in the light of conditions prevailing in Kuwait itself. The Mission has given careful consideration to the present school curricula. In many respects they are admirable, but the Mission believes that the following observations should be considered.

Primary Schools. Primary education is fundamental. Taking into account the nature of the learner, the problem of living in Kuwait and the fact that formal primary education there is only four years, it should aim to achieve:

a) mastery of the basic tools of reading, writing and arithmetic;

b) the establishment of good habits which are essential for the physical health of the child;

c) the imparting of a minimum of geographical and historical information about Kuwait and neighboring countries; and

d) development in the child of the feeling of belonging to his own group.

Virtually no geography or history, however, is given before the fourth year of the primary school, when the student is about ten years old. Study of geography and history could very well start earlier and be taught in one unit. Nature study should receive more attention in the fourth year. Arabic teaching, especially the grammar, seems to cover items not readily grasped at this stage. Simplification is needed.

Intermediate Schools. Students in the last two years of the intermediate school are approaching adolescence. Although psychologically there is no sharp line dividing the various stages of the physical, emotional and mental development of the individual, there are certain factors which characterize each stage. One of the main characteristics of students at the secondary level is the individual's desire to know more about himself. Therefore, the study of elementary physiology should receive some attention. Another important characteristic is the desire of the student to do manual work. This is an ideal time for practical work to be introduced and emphasized. Therefore, much more attention should be given to handwork. We think that in the girls' intermediate school more time is needed for home economics.

Academic Secondary Schools. Due to the importance of science in modern life, we recommend an increase in the number of weekly periods in the natural sciences, chemistry, physics and biology. Sociology could very well be deleted from the first two years and covered in the last two years of the literary section, or at least incorporated in history, which is taught in the first two years.

Vocational Education. Education in Kuwait has so far failed by a wide margin in training the required number of skilled workers for industry and commerce. It has also failed to attract an adequate number of students for practical studies, whether at home or abroad. We understand some of the factors involved. Not only in Kuwait itself, but in most of the Arab countries interest in vocational training is still weak. A number of circumstances have contributed to this undesirable situation, such as the shortage of specialists in vocational education and unfamiliarity with modern machinery.

Kuwait has made some progress in vocational training in recent years. But the need to guide students, especially in the intermediate school, toward vocational education is great. As the number of students increases, and, hopefully, the employment in government offices decreases, some in the intermediate schools will, of course, have no alternative but to explore other avenues for study besides education leading to office work. Due to the fact that vocational education is so essential for the economy of Kuwait, we recommend the establishment of an advisory committee on this subject. This committee may be composed of representatives from the Chamber of Commerce, KOC and the Ministries of Public Works, Education and Social Affairs. One of the main functions of such a committee would be to consider ways and means to arouse interest in vocational education and to advise on its scope and direction.

In the following paragraphs the Mission comments briefly on the two existing vocational schools.

1) *The Commercial School.* In respect to the evening commercial school now operating, the 1961 Mission recommended that the commercial section be separated from the academic secondary school and another commercial school at the secondary level be opened. We are glad to note that such a school is starting this year. Commerce is still the principal vocation in Kuwait. We are confident that a commercial school at the secondary level will be very favorably received. Evening courses already established, both for government employees and private employees, should be continued and enlarged.

2) *The Technical College.* The Technical College is of good standing. However, we suggest that in the near future the college should admit only intermediate school graduates. If this suggestion is adopted, technical education will be more on a par with the academic secondary education. The technical graduates will be more competent and mature. The psychological effect of having a technical college of the same level as that of the academic secondary school would be extremely important. Technical education should relate its program directly to the actual needs and demands of the Kuwait economy. Trained workers in air conditioning, radio repair, electrical appliances, auto mechanics and building materials are in great demand. The Technical College should take this into consideration and plan its program accordingly. A beginning in petroleum technology should also be introduced. Petroleum engineering, geology and chemistry are usually given at the university level. However, the study of the mechanical aspects of the industry could begin at the secondary level. Cooperation with the KOC (which already provides training in the field) and other oil companies in Kuwait is

highly desirable. Attention should also be given to training in marine trades, in view of the interest of Kuwaitis in the sea and the need for crews to man the tanker fleet under the Kuwaiti flag. Home economics training at the secondary level should be provided for girls, with emphasis on domestic science, home management and child care.

Examinations. Advancement in an educational career should be on the basis of measured achievements. An examination, whatever form it takes—oral or written, practical or theoretical—is one kind of measurement. Until recent times, written tests were unduly emphasized in most educational systems. That was understandable, as the earlier concept of education was based simply on the acquisition of knowledge and skills. Modern education emphasizes cultural and social development as well. In the light of this, the scope of evaluation has been broadened, and examinations of the old type are not enough.

The Mission feels that too many students are failed in the primary grades. Although the percentage of failures is decreasing, it is still high. In 1959/60 only about 70 per cent of the pupils in the fourth year of the urban primary schools passed. In rural primary schools, failures are more numerous than in the urban schools.

The Mission realizes that high standards of scholarship must be maintained. But there should not be a rigid policy of placing exclusive emphasis on final examinations. In the primary school there should be few failures. The emphasis should be on guidance. Cumulative records of the student's growth—mentally and socially—should be introduced, and promotions should take place on this basis. If guidance is seriously applied in the intermediate schools and students' interests are taken into consideration, the percentage of failures at that level will probably be appreciably decreased.

Discipline. Education should be conducted in a favorable atmosphere. Discipline in school is prerequisite for achieving that end, and lack of it may be a factor in student failures. While students need a sympathetic approach by school administrators and teachers with an absence of harshness and rigidity, yet softness and uncontrolled freedom are harmful to academic progress. As a result of its school visits and meetings with headmasters and teachers, the Mission concluded that discipline is lacking in some cases. The 1963 Mission was informed that those failing twice are dropped from school. This is hardly a substitute for day-to-day discipline.

Teacher Training

The lack of well-trained Kuwaiti teachers is the most important problem in education Kuwait is facing. As we have already seen, 95 per cent of teachers in Kuwait are non-Kuwaitis. At present Kuwaitis are not inclined to follow teaching as a career, and certainly the teachers recruited from abroad have faithfully discharged their duties. But the non-Kuwaiti teachers, a number of whom have been in Kuwait [for ten years or more, feel insecure. If the Kuwaiti authorities are satisfied with the services of such teachers, granting them nationality on a preferred basis should be seriously considered. It is unlikely that Kuwait will be able in the near future to train an adequate number of Kuwaitis to staff all the existing schools and those to be opened in the future.

Special efforts should also be made to train Kuwaitis for teaching in their own schools. It is a pity to expose small children to teachers from so many countries. In 1961, Kuwait had already opened the Women's Teacher Training School where girls were trained for teaching in the kindergarten and the primary schools. While a three-year course after intermediate school, which is provided now, may be adequate at this stage, it is advisable to raise it as soon as possible to a four-year course. The present policy of encouraging girls to enter the teaching profession is good. In addition, the Ministry of Education has now established a Men's Teacher Training School.

Attracting students to teaching is difficult but not impossible. Although an appreciable number of secondary school teachers and instructors for the teacher-training schools can be trained through government scholarships abroad, the overwhelming majority of teachers for the kindergarten, primary and intermediate schools will have to be trained in Kuwait itself. The gradually increasing number of secondary school graduates and a policy of greater selectivity for study abroad should help to ease the problem of recruitment for the teacher training schools. A two-year professional course for training intermediate school teachers should be established for some of the secondary school graduates who receive no government scholarships for study abroad. The adoption of such a measure is imperative.

Money is always a strong incentive. Therefore, the 1961 Mission proposed that teachers' salaries should compare favorably with salaries of government officials having the same qualifications. We are glad to note that this proposal has now been put into effect. In addition, promising teachers should be selected and sent abroad for higher education and specialization, and they should be promoted on their return.

Another problem is that at least 50 per cent of the present non-Kuwaiti teachers are not professionally trained. A large portion of them are only graduates of secondary schools or the equivalent. A number have had some professional courses, but that is not adequate. We suggest that a summer school for newly recruited non-Kuwaiti teachers who are only secondary school graduates or the equivalent should be opened in a neighboring country, such as Lebanon, to give a professional course of from 8 to 12 weeks. Evening courses for teachers should be given throughout the year. The 1963 Mission was informed of considerable progress in providing in-service teacher training.

The facilities now available in Kuwait train Kuwaiti teachers for the kindergarten and the primary schools. The intermediate and secondary schools should not be overlooked. Teaching in the intermediate school needs as thorough a preparation as teaching in the secondary school—that is, a college degree or its equivalent. At present, however, a two-year course after secondary schooling might be adequate. Therefore, we suggest the establishment in the next few years of two professional schools, one for girls and the other for boys, where teachers for the intermediate school can be trained. Both these professional schools should provide at least a two-year course after secondary education. The establishment of such a higher college for training secondary school teachers should be one of the first specialized faculties opened in the proposed Kuwait university. Should the establishment of the proposed university be long delayed we recommend the opening of a higher teachers college to be incorporated later in the university when it is established.

The success of all the proposed teacher-training centers depends in part on the facilities for observation and practice teaching. The Mission strongly advises that a kindergarten, primary or intermediate school, as the case may be, should be attached to each of the teacher-training centers for observation, practice teaching and research. The contribution of demonstration schools to the preparation of well qualified teachers can hardly be over-emphasized. It is an accepted procedure to consider demonstration schools as part of the teachers' training school itself.

Educational Planning and Research. Planning is an important attribute of modern life. In educational planning, the Government should assess the need for education in the total life of the country.

Alongside the national economic plan, there ought to be a national educational plan. The Ministry of Education is aware of the necessity of having a practical and sound educational plan. Hence, it has endeavored to obtain advice from abroad. Recently, it has been working on a five-year plan. Regardless of how good and realistic the plan is, it will have to be revised from time to time. Instead of making this revision under the press of circumstances, it is advisable to have a small unit within the Ministry charged with the over-all planning of education. This unit should also engage in research and study of teaching methods and materials suitable for Kuwait. The person in charge of this unit should have under his jurisdiction the collection and analysis of educational statistics.

School Inspection. Regardless of how reliable and well trained the teachers are, they need continuous guidance from persons who are more mature and professionally competent. The Ministry of Education has engaged a large number of persons for school supervision. The effectiveness of the supervisors has been reduced considerably, however, because virtually all of them are carrying on routine administrative work in the Ministry. To illustrate: A supervisor who had the responsibility to look after only 150 teachers (some inspectors are responsible for supervising the work of 250) was unable to visit all of those assigned to him. Unless a teacher is visited a number of times a year, and each visit is of reasonable length, school supervision will fail to achieve its aim. If the supervisors are relieved from their routine administrative jobs they will be in a better position not only to visit and guide classroom teachers, but also to conduct seminars, workshops, and lectures for teachers who were recruited with little professional training. The 1963 Mission was informed that some progress has been made in relieving inspectors of administrative tasks.

Higher Education

Establishing a University in Kuwait. Leadership is needed in administration, education, other professions and commerce. A leader needs to be a well educated person, with specialization and excellence in at least one area of endeavor. Specialization is provided at the college or university level. But this is not the only function of a university. A university should play a major role in the preservation and the development of the national culture. The services of a first-class university should not, of course, be limited to the country where it is located. From such a point of view, the establishment of a university in any country is desirable. But a number of factors have to be considered before a final decision is taken on the establishment of such an institution in Kuwait.

Reference has already been made to the study of the University Advisory Commission. The Commission proposed that the existing boys' secondary school building could be altered to serve as a university building, and recommended the pattern for the proposed Kuwait University. The availability of students and funds, the scale and extent of contributions that a university would make both inside and outside the country, and the availability of a teaching and research staff, however, are still to be considered.

The 1961 Mission felt that if the university were started about 1965, as was then planned, one could envisage the enrollment of about 700 students. Actually the number of students in secondary schools now is much greater than in 1961 (about double in the senior year). The view seems to be widely held in Kuwait, however, that a university would not attract many undergraduates, since students would much prefer to go abroad on government scholarships. The 1963 Mission was informed that the matter was still under consideration.

The following are the considerations that led the 1961 Mission to generally favor some sort of institution of higher learning in Kuwait:

a) Kuwait unquestionably is financially capable of establishing a university of high standing, which would seem to have a higher priority than, say, the purchase of land. Besides, as the University Advisory Commission said, the present boys' secondary school building and those which are occupied by the Technical College could very well house the proposed university with some alterations and additions. Kuwait could follow this suggestion, or choose another site and ask some consulting firm to draw a plan for a desired university layout. So far as money and buildings are concerned, there is no problem.

b) In dealing with the value of the institution, we should remember that approximately one-fourth of the school population is non-Kuwaiti. The Arab provinces of the Gulf are relying more and more on Kuwait for education. Kuwait has responded magnificently. Not only has it opened schools in the Gulf, but it has also provided an appreciable number of scholarships to non-Kuwaitis in schools in Kuwait itself. The number of non-Kuwaitis graduating from the secondary schools, run by the Ministry of Education both inside and outside Kuwait, is definitely likely to increase year by year. Other countries in the area, although they may have institutions of higher learning, might send some of their students to a Kuwait university of sufficient quality and stature. Awarding scholarships to non-Kuwaitis would be a strong incentive.

c) In the absence of an institution of higher learning in Kuwait, sending secondary school graduates abroad would have to continue for years to come. The advantages of sending nationals to foreign countries are readily admitted. Competence in one field or another is gained, and students have the opportunity of familiarizing themselves with another culture. But there are also some risks in sending young people of a secondary school level abroad. Confusion and bewilderment are not unlikely. Some of them not only find it difficult to adjust themselves overseas, but are unable to fit themselves into their own country upon their return. The present high incidence of failures of Kuwaitis studying abroad may be indicative of the danger of dispatching immature students abroad with plentiful spending money. There are advantages in training most of one's people at home.

d) The fourth and perhaps most important point is whether Kuwait is in a position to provide or engage the nucleus of a university staff. At this stage, Kuwait depends almost entirely on non-Kuwaitis even for elementary and secondary instructors. The number of Kuwaitis who have been sent abroad for higher education is not small, but probably not many of them will come back with the idea of joining the staff of the university, even assuming that they could meet the required qualifications. Therefore, the university would have to depend primarily on staff drawn from the Middle East and western countries during at least the first ten years of its life. Difficult as it is, the problem of recruiting of the teaching staff does not seem insoluble. Rewards in terms of salaries, research equipment and amenities would have to be substantial. At the same time, a well planned program of study abroad can be organized to train Kuwaitis for teaching at the university.

The 1963 Mission, for its part, also feels that Kuwait should have some facility for higher education. A university may be composed of various faculties, such as arts and sciences, engineering, medicine, pharmacy, law, and the like. Practicality and need should determine which faculty should be established first. Doctors, engineers, skilled workers, teachers, all are needed, but these needs should be arranged in a list of priorities. The Mission would also emphasize that sound scientific and literary education should either precede or accompany professional training.

A number of professional schools and research institutes have been suggested for Kuwait. It is assumed that they would form part of the university if it were established. In fact, they might well be established as steps toward a full-fledged university.

The Higher Teachers' College. We have already stated that a professional teachers' college for training secondary school staff should be established as soon as possible after the university question is settled, or even before. If students enter directly from secondary school, a four- or five-year course would be required. The program for the first two years should be the same for all students. In the third and subsequent years it should be feasible to divide the student body into two sections, scientific and literary. We suggest that the main areas of specialization to be elected after the second year should be mathematics and physics, biology and chemistry, social studies, Arabic study and foreign languages and the professional courses. Each student should have a major and a minor. For example, mathematics may be the major field of a student and physics his minor. The course and the areas of studies will have to be dealt with in detail by specialists. We suggest, however, that the professional courses should constitute from one-fourth to one-fifth of the total program. If the university with the usual liberal arts curriculum is established, its graduates, or graduates of comparable standing from universities outside Kuwait, should be given a two-year course at the teachers' training college for professional teacher-training.

Arid Zone Institute. A proposal has been made to set up in Kuwait a research and training institute to concentrate on the problems of arid zones. The proposal is laudable, but it may be pointed out that the field is vast, the problems large and multifarious. If the idea is to conduct research on desert agriculture, then the Agricultural Farm could be strengthened with some research scholars and laboratory equipment. If, on the other hand, the institute is to deal with larger problems, then the Mission suggests that it would be advisable to communicate with Unesco, which has undertaken a number of studies since 1950 on arid zones. The Government might ask Unesco for an expert who would advise on the proposed institute and the fields it would cover, and who would provide any literature available on the subject. It may be pointed out that the United Arab Republic has established a "General Desert Development Authority" which also looks after the Egyptian Desert Institute. The Government of Iraq has established an Arid Zone Research Institute in the College of Agriculture at Abu Gharib. It would be pointless to duplicate the studies undertaken at these institutions. It is therefore imperative that the fields for study be carefully chosen, because an arid zone institute should be an asset for the entire region and not only useful for Kuwait.

Petroleum Institute. The Ministry of Education informed the 1961 Mission that it was considering the establishment of a petroleum institute. We assume that the objectives of the institute would be (1) to educate experts to work in the petroleum industry and to advise the Government of Kuwait; (2) to keep abreast of modern developments in the petroleum industry and establish a reference library; and (3) to carry out research into problems of the industry peculiar to Kuwait and the Middle East.

The Mission agrees that it is desirable to have experts available who are abreast of latest developments in the field. For this reason, it would be preferable to train Kuwaitis for this task, and a beginning should be made with vocational training in the Technical College. There are three main facets of the more advanced study of petroleum, i.e., petroleum geology, petroleum engineering and petroleum chemistry. Each of these are fields in themselves. It would be appropriate for a student interested in taking up petroleum as his career to have enough knowledge of all three by the time he graduates from college to be able to choose one for his post graduate work. For a number of years to come, a university in Kuwait is not likely to be equipped to give such advanced training. The Mission suggests that the Ministry of Education, when it feels the caliber of general science training at the university is up to advanced study, should ask for technical advice from abroad on graduate study in petroleum. The University of Oklahoma in the United States is regarded as an outstanding institution in the field. Its course of study as well as those of other universities of repute in petroleum studies should be consulted.

Management of the University. Coordination between the Ministry of Education and the university will be a matter of great importance. Countries differ in their approach to this problem. In England and the United States, for example, universities are largely independent.

In other countries such as France, United Arab Republic and Iraq, the Ministries of Education assume the responsibility for coordinating and planning of all educational activities, including higher education. It is for the Kuwait Government to decide on the pattern of coordination and administration. In newly emerging nations, however, a strong tie between university and the government agency responsible for over-all planning and execution of the educational program is advisable. But whatever the form of coordination, it should never mean detailed interference by government in academic matters.

Adult Education

Kuwait's achievements in adult education do not compare favorably with its regular education program. Although no statistics are available, the majority of the adult population are probably still illiterate. Although there were 19 centers for male adult education in 1961, with about 3,500 men attending, there were none for women.

The importance of adult education, however, has been recognized by the authorities. While the Ministry of Social Affairs is responsible for the execution of the program, Education, Health and Social Affairs have combined efforts in the planning and execution of the program. Nevertheless, a more comprehensive approach is urgently needed. The Mission suggests the establishment of an advisory committee with representatives from government agencies such as the Ministries of Social Affairs, Education, Health and Labor and private organizations. The main functions of such an advisory committee would be to (1) draw up an over-all plan for adult education, (2) decide on the specific responsibilities of each agency, government or private, (3) consider ways and means to obtain local participation, (4) formulate a plan for training workers in the general field of adult education, and (5) assess progress achieved and recommend the introduction of needed modifications.

The plan for adult education which we have in mind includes the following:

a) *Combating Illiteracy*. Being a small country with spacious schools, Kuwait is in an excellent position to plan and execute a comprehensive program for the eradication of illiteracy among its adult population. In combating adult illiteracy, books different from those used in teaching children are needed. Excellent books of the right kind have been produced in the Sudan and the United Arab Republic; and Kuwait could very well use these. Teaching people how to read and write is simply one part of the whole task. Every adult in the community, in order to be a useful member, should be provided with the general information which a citizen needs. Every adult should know the minimum essentials of health, skills, and be informed about the history and geography of his own country.

b)   *Community Development.* In many countries, especially in undeveloped areas, programs are drawn up to improve conditions on a community basis. There are a few communities in Kuwait where this could be done. A team approach might be followed, with one member of the team competent in combating illiteracy, another in child care, another in home economics, and so on. The aim should be to draw the attention of the people to shortcomings in their respective communities, to create interest and to encourage cooperation in improving conditions. A main objective should be to provide advice and organize leadership. A number of centers are found in the Arab nations for training social workers. For example, the Kuwait Government could send persons for training to the Sirs El-Layyan Center in the United Arab Republic.

c)   *Leisure.* The proper utilization of leisure time has become a real issue in modern society, particularly in wealthy communities such as Kuwait. The economic changes which have taken place during the last decade have tremendously affected the social life of the people. They have now more leisure time than ever before, and the old forms of recreation are insufficient. Opening of fundamental education centers and clubs are some of the measures which have been taken. What has been done so far is good. However, the Mission feels that more adequate facilities for sea bathing are needed (contractors have largely denuded the beaches of sand), and salt-water swimming pools could be easily constructed. More athletic fields and encouraging the establishment of more clubs, athletic as well as social, is strongly recommended. The recreational value of the cinema should not be underestimated. The need for more cinemas is obvious and the present monopoly is neither necessary nor desirable. The Government has made good use of the Kuwait Broadcasting Station as a medium for recreation and education.

d) Further Suggestions. Kuwait may, with advantage, consider
other projects in the field of general culture. The Ministry
of Education already has a detailed recommendation to enlarge
the Kuwait Museum facilities, and we endorse the recommendation. The publication of Arab manuscripts, the translation
of famous Arab books, and the academy of music also require
consideration.

A large number of public and private libraries, the world
over, have opened sections for Arab manuscripts. Many of
these manuscripts, however, are still not accessible to the
public. The Arab League has recently created a section in
its Cultural Department charged with microfilming manuscripts
and books. This section has done valuable work, but its
contribution should be supplemented. Kuwait, being an Arab
nation, is in a very favorable position to give a helping hand
in the collection and publication of Arab manuscripts.

During the medieval period, as well as in recent centuries,
Arab scholars contributed much to science and letters. Many
Arab books have gained world-wide reputations, but only a few
have been translated into well-known foreign languages. It
would be a major contribution to human understanding if
some of these manuscripts and books were translated into
English, French or other foreign languages. A commission
of scholars could be formed to whom the choice of books and
manuscripts for translation would be entrusted. Individual
scholars should be engaged to do the translation.

Love of the arts and music is part of the Arab tradition.
Music received attention during the Abbasid Dynasty in
Baghdad and that of Omaayads in Spain. The names of a great
number of Arab singers and musicians are still remembered,
even by illiterate Arabs. Arab music has acquired its own pattern during the ages. Recently some revival of Arab music has
taken place, especially in the United Arab Republic. Kuwait
has started the collection of Arab folk songs and old Arab
musical instruments. The project is still in its embryonic stage
and should be encouraged.

Projected School Construction Program

The Ministry of Education has projected an ambitious school
construction program during the three years ending March 31, 1965.

This program contemplates the construction of 51 new schools at a cost of KD 24.6 million.

At present, the school population seems to be increasing a little faster than classroom space, and the number of students per classroom ranges from 37 for primary to 30 for secondary schools. The need for additional classrooms seems apparent. The 1961 Mission felt, however, that the need for school construction at the rate then contemplated for the five-year period 1961–65 was not very well established. The program then envisaged 64 new schools for this period. However, only 13 of these schools have been finished in the last two years leaving 51 still to be completed in this and the following two years. This would involve an expenditure of over KD 8 million a year in these three years— more than twice the amount spent in 1962/63. In any event an increase in the number of school units by about 35 per cent in three years, even granted that one or two of these are specialized facilities, does not seem necessary. Even in Kuwait the population of school age is unlikely to increase at this rate.

It is planned to open 15 kindergartens in the coming three years. We are of the opinion that this plan should be extended over at least five years. It seems to be possible and desirable to open three kindergartens a year. In 1961, the Department of Education estimated that there will be approximately 2,700 children applying for admission to the kindergarten each year. Taking into account that there are now about 8,000 children in the 24 kindergartens, or about 330 per kindergarten, and that approximately 2,000 of them will be going to the primary school, new places will have to be found for about 700 children. In the coming years, this number is likely to increase gradually. If we assume that each kindergarten will accommodate about 300 children, an average of three kindergartens a year seems to be adequate, even assuming some reduction in students per class.

It is planned to open 17 primary schools during the coming three years; that is, on the average, nearly six primary schools each year. The 1961 Mission felt that four or five rather than six schools a year would be required. However, another review of the primary school enrollments in recent years makes it appear that the six schools a year target is not unreasonable.

From 1963 to 1965, it is planned to open ten intermediate schools and seven secondary schools. It is our impression that this may result in some overbuilding of intermediate and secondary school facilities. Even if the present secondary school for boys is taken over by the proposed university, the suggested seven new secondary schools are more than likely to be needed during this period. This question should be carefully considered in the light of the number of students in the intermediate school. The new teacher-training school and the new commercial school are necessary, however. The 1961 Mission was doubtful about the need for a secondary agricultural school and marine school. As far as is known, these are not now in the program.

APPENDIX 1
NATIONAL PRODUCT OF KUWAIT, 1959 and 1962/63

No official national income calculations of any kind have been made for Kuwait, and the available statistical information allows only very approximate estimates of the national accounts. Data for disposable gross income presented in the tables at the end of this Appendix correspond approximately to the concept of Gross National Product. It is not possible to produce net figures except for oil revenues and other external transactions. No distinction has been made between estimates in market prices and in factor costs.

Three sectors are discussed: The private sector, the Government, and foreign countries. The "foreign countries" sector includes the operations of the foreign oil companies even if they are conducted partly within the borders of Kuwait. The income of the oil companies after tax is disposed of by the foreign owners of the companies, and does not directly affect the economy. Another possible treatment of the after-tax income of the oil companies would consist of computing the value of Gross Domestic Product, including the total value of oil production, and then subtracting the oil companies' share to arrive at net national income. However, the actual value of oil production is not available.

The "foreign countries" account (Column (4) of the tables) is based largely on the estimate of the Kuwait balance of payments contained in Chapter 5. The expenditures of the foreign sector include the payments of oil revenues to the Government and the oil companies' expenditures for local labor and materials. The Government's "income from production" consists of the oil revenues. The income from production for the private sector will be explained below.

The factor income receipts from abroad were obtained from the government accounts for the government sector. For the private sector the figure is a pure estimate based on a very rough indication of the private foreign investments of Kuwait.

The Gross National Product estimates of KD 296 million for 1959 and KD 370 million for 1962/63 would indicate an average growth of about 8 per cent a year. However, if our population estimates are approximately correct, per capita GNP may have decreased from about KD 1,142 ($3,138) in 1959 to KD 1,057 ($2,960) in 1962/63.

The disposition of the gross government disposable income and the financial investment of the private sector were estimated from official fiscal and monetary data and from the balance of payments estimates of the Mission. Difficult problems arise, however, in estimating the gross income of the private sector, owing to lack of statistics. A different approach to this problem was taken for 1962/63 than for 1959 because of the availability of some new data in the later year.

For 1959 we first estimated the net income paid to the private sector by the government sector and from abroad (i.e., the oil companies and from foreign investments). This amounted to KD 119 million, consisting of government expenditures in the economy (KD 67 million), proceeds of government land purchases net of internal taxes (KD 45 million), and local expenditures of the oil companies (KD 7 million). We then applied to this a multiplier of 1.5, arriving at a gross disposable income for the private sector rounded to KD 181 million.[1] The income from production figure of KD 143 million was then calculated as a residual, since the other sources of income were already estimated separately.

For 1962/63, the income from production figure of KD 195 million was estimated directly.[2] It is made up of KD 160 million of compensation to employees, KD 25 million of business profits and KD 10 million

[1] The multiplier will depend upon the average propensities to save (in excess of domestic capital outlays), and to import. Total net private financial investment (savings in excess of domestic investment) was KD 47 million, as shown in Column 1, KD 27 million of foreign investment plus KD 20 million increase in bank deposits in Kuwait (net of bank credit expansion to the private sector). In addition, transfers of non-Kuwaitis to abroad are estimated at KD 11 million. This makes a total of KD 58 million, which gives us a rough order of magnitude of private domestic "savings" exclusive of private capital outlays in Kuwait. Net private imports, obtained by deducting goods imported for the Government from total imports, were about KD 73 million in 1959. Comparing these two amounts, i.e., KD 58 million and KD 73 million, and taking account of the large margin of error that is bound to be present, we may conclude that the average propensity to "save" and to import were roughly of the same order of magnitude. The question remains as to what portion they represent of the gross income (product) of the private sector. From observation, the Mission guessed that the import content in private expenditures was about 50 per cent. Therefore, we concluded that savings, expenditures on imports and expenditures on domestic goods and services absorb roughly equal portions of gross disposable income of the private sector. Thus the savings and import "leakages" together would amount to two-thirds and the income multiplier would be 1.5.

[2] If the same technique had been used for 1962/63 as for 1959, the gross disposable income estimate would have been about KD 226 million rather than KD 215 million.

from rents, etc.[3] The estimate for business profits was based on about a 25 per cent mark-up on imports, and the rental income is based on information received from the Ministry of Social Affairs and Labor.

In both years the breakdown between consumption and capital outlays was made by estimating capital outlays by multiplying capital goods imports by 2.5 (assuming 40:60 ratio between materials and labor) and calculating consumption as a residual.

The Mission is of the opinion that the data for gross income and savings may be reasonably accurate. The increase in consumption between 1959 and 1962/63 is smaller than might be expected. It is noteworthy, however, that despite the increase in population, retained imports—a good indication of consumption in Kuwait—increased only by about KD 8 million as between these two years. We suspect, however, that disposable income in the private sector may have been somewhat higher than KD 215 million in 1962/63 and that consumption was correspondingly larger than this table indicates.

[3] Of the KD 160 million of compensation to employees, KD 53 million was the amount provided for personnel (including our estimate of the amount paid to the armed forces which is not specified in the budget) in the current budget. Compensation to private sector employees is a very rough estimate based mostly on the registration of the non-Kuwaiti labor force, referred to in Chapter 4, and observed levels of pay for different classes of labor. We assumed that professionals and business employees received an average of KD 2,000 a year, skilled workers KD 750 and unskilled KD 300. These figures are roughly in line with the government wage scale and correspond to information given the Mission by private employers. For the Kuwaiti labor force (estimated at 20,000 in the private sector) we assumed that half averaged KD 2,000 a year and half KD 750. The computation is as follows:

	Number	Assumed Average Annual Income (KD)	Income (KD Million)
Non-Kuwaiti—			
Business and Professional	16,000	2,000	32
Non-Kuwaiti Skilled	47,000	750	35
Non-Kuwaiti Unskilled	42,000	300	13
Kuwaiti—Business and Professional	10,000	2,000	20
Other Kuwaiti	10,000	750	7
Government Employees			53
			160

ESTIMATED NATIONAL ACCOUNTS, 1959 [a]

(KD Million)

	(1) Private	(2) Kuwait Government	(3) Total	(4) Foreign (Including Oil Co's)
Income from Production [b]	143	150	293	(157)
Factor Income Receipts from Abroad	4	10	14	(14)
Factor Income Payments to Abroad	(11)		(11)	11
Gross National Product	136	160	296	(160)
Transfers (Land Sales less Internal Taxes)	45	(45)	—	
Gross Disposable Income	181	115	296	
Disposition				
(1) Consumption	(101)	(62)	(163)	91)
(2) Capital Outlays	(33)	(33)	(63)	
(3) Financial Investment	(47)[c]	(23)[d]	(70)	69[e]
(4) Savings (2) + (4)	(80)	(53)	(133)	
Total (1) + (4)	(181)	(115)	(296)	160
Savings as Per Cent of Disposable Income	44	46	45	

[a] Figures not in parentheses are receipts; in parentheses are payments.

[b] Not including the retained share of the oil companies; if this were added, one would obtain Gross Domestic Product.

[c] Private remittances (KD 34 million) plus reinvestment of factor income receipts from abroad (KD 4 million) minus factor income payments to abroad (KD 11 million) plus net increase in private deposits in Kuwait banks (KD 20 million).

[d] Net increase in official foreign assets (KD 25 million) minus decrease in government deposits in Kuwait banks (KD 3 million).

[e] Private remittances (KD 34 million) less factor payments abroad (KD 11 million) plus increase in official foreign assets (KD 25 million) plus increase in foreign assets of banks (KD 17 million) plus factor income receipts from abroad (KD 4 million).

Note: Theoretically, total financial investment (KD 70 million) should equal total foreign investment (KD 69 million). The difference is a statistical discrepancy.

ESTIMATED NATIONAL ACCOUNTS, 1962/63 [a]

(KD Million)

	(1) Private	(2) Kuwait Government	(3) Total	(4) Foreign (Including Oil Co's)
Income from Production [b]	195	173	368	(190)
Factor Income Receipts from Abroad	10	12	22	(22)
Factor Income Payments to Abroad	(20)		(20)	20
Gross National Product	185	185	370	(192)
Transfers (Land Sales less Internal Taxes	30	(30)	—	
Gross Disposable Income	215	155	370	
Disposition				
(1) Consumption	(107)	(93)	(200)	95
(2) Capital Outlays	(35)	(35)	(70)	
(3) Financial Investment	(73)[c]	(27)[d]	(100)	97[e]
(4) Savings (2) + (3)	(103)	(62)	(170)	
Total (1) + (4)	(215)	(155)	(370)	192
Savings as Per Cent of Disposable Income	50	41	46	

[a] Figures not in parentheses are receipts; in parentheses are payments.

[b] Not including the retained share of the oil companies.

[c] Private capital movements (KD 77 million) plus net increase in private monetary factors (KD 6 million) less factor payments abroad (KD 20 million) plus reinvestment of factor income receipts from abroad (KD 10 million).

[d] Net increase in official foreign assets (KD 33 million) minus decrease in government deposits in Kuwait (KD 6 million).

[e] Private capital movements (KD 77 million) plus increase in official foreign assets (KD 33 million) less factor payments abroad (KD 20 million) plus reinvestment of private foreign factor income (KD 10 million) minus decrease in foreign assets of banks (KD 3 million).

Note: Theoretically total financial investment (KD 100 million) should equal financial transfers to the foreign sector (KD 97 million). The difference is a statistical discrepancy.

APPENDIX 2 *EXPLORATION FOR WATER*

Water from Damman Formation, Southwest Kuwait

The outcrop region of this Eocene limestone is vast, and substantial water probably has moved down into Kuwait from the overlying sands and gravels. In this connection, the valley of Wadi-el-Batin should be explored by drilling a line of exploratory holes across the valley along with the testing of the underlying limestone. Testing might be done with diesel electric units and submersible pumps from which aquifer coefficients could be evaluated and final schemes designed. Preliminary information indicates that a lift of the order of 167 meters will be required. Discovery of oil or gas in southwestern Kuwait could provide cheaper power and thus reduce the cost of irrigation schemes in that area. Soils anywhere south and west of Kuwait City would probably be amenable to irrigation if above the littoral and away from the outcrops of the marine beds of the lower Fars formation, but a soil survey and research in types of crops and methods of farming would be necessary early in the development. An important early evaluation should be based on complete chemical analyses, particularly for boron.

The cost of producing water near the southwestern corner of Kuwait or along the Wadi Batin (Saudi Arabia) frontier would consist chiefly of the capital investment and operating cost of lifting the water to the surface of the land, plus whatever piping might be required. Gravity flow could be used in most cases, especially if water were developed in the southwestern quadrant of the country and its use were in the environs of Kuwait City. If water were developed on a modest scale, say, 6 million gallons per day from four wells, the diesel electric plant and submersible pump to lift water 167 meters would require a capital investment of about KD 75,000, exclusive of any pipeline needed to transfer water to the irrigated land. This plant would irrigate about 600 hectares and would furnish a basis for estimating costs of larger-scale irrigation schemes. If a welded steel line, 24 inches in diameter were used to pipe the water, cost would be about KD 20,000 per kilometer, including trenching, welding, wrapping, testing and backfilling. Cement asbestos pipe of the same diameter would cost KD 11,200 per kilometer without shipping and installation costs. If the pipe were manufactured in Kuwait, shipping costs would be saved and installation costs would be considerably less than for steel pipe. Thus if 110 kilometers be considered a maximum distance, and the cost KD 15,000 per kilometer, the capital investment for the piping would be on the order of KD 1,650,000 for the pipeline which would deliver about 6 million gallons per day by gravity flow in a cement-asbestos pipe. Allowing 10 per cent for interest and depreciation, this would mean a cost of about 87 fils (24¢) per 1,000 gallons. The total capital cost per hectare of irrigated land would be KD 2,900.

Dibdibba and Kuwait Group

A search should be made behind known structural highs, utilizing the knowledge gained from the Raudhatain field. Axes of structural highs are shown in Map 1. In the event that substantial underflow is found in the valley of Wadi-el-Batin in southwestern Kuwait, the underground channel or channels should be explored further north, particularly south and west of the Mutriba high. A southern extension of the Rumaila high in Iraq is another favorable prospecting area. The northeastern corner of the country should also be tested by shallow exploratory drilling on the theory that there may be some underflow on the flanks of the ancient distributary, Khoras-Zubair.

Further Exploration

It is highly desirable to carry out further explorations to test all possibilities of finding additional fresh water supplies or even of brackish water with low salinity. This could conveniently be combined with a geological and mapping survey of the whole country. The initial step is organization of a governmental unit comparable to geological surveys in other countries. A few competent geologists, engineers and hydrologists should be employed and an intensive mapping program begun. Aerial photographs on a scale of 1:20,000 should be made; the triangulation net developed by the Kuwait Oil Company should be evaluated and perhaps extended and strengthened, utilizing new base-line measuring techniques and tying into geodetic positions in adjoining countries. If the offshore islands cannot be accurately located in this manner, then the photography should be taken with shoran or hiran control to furnish a first-order geodetic control net. An international photogrammetric company should be required to utilize the best available lens, checked against international standards, with the objective of producing large-scale photo maps covering the country. An excellent, although expensive, way would be to use the newly developed orthophoto-scope which would produce photographs rectified to orthographic projection. These may be mosaiced into quadrangles and utilized as plane metric maps which can in turn serve as base maps for topography, geology, soil types, land ownership, international and concession boundaries, etc. This procedure would result in the highest-quality maps for all purposes.

Concurrently with the mapping program, a test-drilling program should be started, utilizing a few rotary-type rigs equipped to take cores and make drill-stem tests. Electrical logging, preferably by a commercial logging company, should be utilized, the objective being to get complete information from every hole not only for hydrologic purposes but for other possible natural resources such as building materials. Adequate office, laboratory and storage facilities will be needed. Such work will become fundamental during development, as quantitative evaluation, particularly hydrologic, will require accurate and detailed information.

STATISTICAL ANNEX

TABLE I: Public Revenues   (KD Million)

	Actual						Budget Estimates
	1957	1958	1959	1960/61	1961/62	1962/63	1963/64
External Sources	117.04	136.20	159.43	169.01	179.05	185.30	195.50
Oil Revenue	110.10	127.32	149.77	159.49	166.94	173.0	183.50
Investment Income	6.94	8.88	9.66	9.52	12.11	12.30	12.00
Internal Sources	5.81	10.31	13.08	14.44	13.84	16.77	12.07
Customs & Ports	1.81	2.05	2.86	4.11	4.38	5.03	3.76
Public Utilities	1.51	2.15	2.89	3.95	3.14	4.05	3.94
Resales of Land	0.26	2.23	2.86	1.93	3.40	4.68	2.49
Miscellaneous	2.19	3.88	4.47	4.45	2.92	3.01	1.38
Total Revenue	122.85	146.51	172.51	183.45	192.89	202.07	208.08

Source: Ministry of Finance.

Note: Totals in this and the following table differ slightly from Table 7 in the text. The latter reflects more recent revisions.

TABLE II: Public Expenditures   (KD Million)

	Actual						Budget Estimates
	1957	1958	1959	1960/61	1961/62	1962/63	1963/64
Amiri	0.41	1.45	2.63	2.66	3.86	3.52	10.00
Defense & Security	8.32	11.24	13.30	16.40	15.00	20.32	22.77
Public Utilities	4.43	5.25	7.22	6.28	7.00	7.69	9.05
Foreign						1.33	3.24
Customs & Port	2.96	3.48	4.44	4.51	4.47	4.29	4.72
Education	9.59	12.93	11.33	8.82	9.02	10.50	13.24
Health	5.09	6.82	6.57	7.75	7.62	8.82	10.21
Guidance						3.31	5.02
Housing	0.94	1.18	1.42	2.01	2.09	2.16	2.47
Municipal	2.66	3.80	3.04	3.29	3.70	5.47	5.15
Others	3.78	4.21	5.20	4.94	13.36	14.31*	13.57
Total "Current"	38.18	50.36	55.21	56.66	67.12	81.71	99.44
Public Works Department	24.09	24.60	23.72	8.73	9.33	8.58	8.28
Construction	4.64	1.47	6.24	26.66	26.34	26.80	42.07
Total "Development"	28.73	26.06	29.96	35.39	35.67	35.38	50.35
Land Purchases	21.91	40.03	58.11	43.03	58.86	46.50	40.00
GRAND TOTAL	88.82	116.45	143.28	135.08	161.65	163.59	189.79

* Includes 4.85 million allocations to "emergency reserve."
Source: Ministry of Finance.

TABLE III: Balance Sheet of Kuwait Currency Board   (KD Million)

	May 17, 1961	Dec. 30, 1961	Dec. 30, 1962	June 30, 1963	Sept. 30, 1963
Assets	25.6	29.9	34.7	35.0	32.4
Foreign Assets	25.6	29.4	34.2	34.8	31.6
Gold	—	15.5	17.5	17.5	15.5
Foreign Government Treasury Bills	—	13.9	16.7	17.3	16.1
Claims on India	25.6	—	—	—	—
Cash (in hand) with Banks	—	0.5	0.5	0.2	0.7
Liabilities	25.6	29.9	34.7	35.0	32.4
Notes and Coin Issue	25.6	29.5	34.0	34.1	31.3
Reserves and Other Liabilities	—	0.4	0.7	0.9	1.1

Source: Kuwait Currency Board and International Monetary Fund, Staff Report on 1962 Consultations with Kuwait.

TABLE IV: Amalgamated Balance Sheet of the Commercial Banks

(KD Million)

	End of					
	1960	1961	1962	March 1963	June 1963	September 1963
Assets						
Cash in Tills	4.1	3.2	3.4	3.5	4.7	3.5
Accounts with Local Banks	0.8	1.0	0.7	1.0	1.3	1.1
Foreign Assets	99.6	137.2	148.7	138.7	136.2	140.4
Advances and Discounts	27.8	28.8	41.6	47.5	51.0	54.4
Other Assets Accounts	0.8	1.4	2.0	1.7	1.9	1.8
Contra Accounts	19.4	26.1	30.1	32.0	28.5	29.7
Total Assets	152.5	197.7	226.6	224.4	223.6	230.9
Liabilities						
Government Deposits	24.0	28.3	26.8	22.3	22.0	24.5
Private Deposits	95.5	120.1	145.5	144.8	145.6	148.1
Foreign Liabilities	0.3	0.3	2.0	2.2	3.2	3.0
Accounts with Local Banks	0.2	0.7	0.7	1.0	1.4	1.0
Capital and Reserve Accounts	4.7	8.9	11.8	11.8	11.8	11.8
Other Liability Accounts	8.4	13.3	9.7	10.3	11.1	12.8
Contra Accounts	19.4	26.1	30.1	32.0	28.5	29.7
Total Liabilities	152.5	197.7	226.6	224.4	223.6	230.9

Source: Kuwait Currency Board and Commercial Banks and International Monetary Fund, Staff Report on 1962 Consultations with Kuwait.

TABLE V: Government Loans

Loans	Disbursement Dates	Amount (KD Million)
Lebanon		
4% Loan to Beirut Municipality	June 10, 1962	2
Repayable on June 10, 1972	July 28, 1963	2
Jordan		
4% Loan Repayable According to	August 2, 1960	0.5
Following Schedule:	December 1, 1960	0.5
August 1, 1963 to 1967: 60,000		
August 1, 1967 to 1968: 100,000		
August 1, 1969 to 1971: 200,000		
Algeria		
Interest-free 25-Year Loan	July 22, 1963	3
	July 30, 1963	2
	July 31, 1963	1
2-Year 6% Loan to Algerian Banks	November 1963	6.5
Iraq		
25-year Interest-free Loan	October 15, 1963	30
United Arab Republic		
15-Year Interest-free Loan	(Obtained on	
Repayable after 1966 in	November 23, 1963)	3
12 Installments		

Source: Ministry of Finance and press reports.

TABLE VI: Destination of Exports of Crude Oil Produced by KOC, 1962

Destination	Million Tons	Per Cent
Western Europe	51.90	63.9
United Kingdom	23.32	28.7
Italy	11.42	14.1
France	7.55	9.3
Holland	6.01	7.4
Germany	1.75	2.2
Other	1.85	2.2
Asia	16.72	20.6
Japan	11.01	13.6
Aden	3.29	4.0
Malaya	2.42	3.0
United States	5.06	6.2
Australia	2.53	3.1
Brazil	1.49	1.8
Egypt	0.90	1.1
Other	2.70	3.3
Total	81.30	100.0

Source: KOC.

TABLE VII: Public Development Allocations and Expenditures   (KD Million)

	(1) Estimated Total Cost of Projects	(2) 1961/62 Allocation	(3) 1961/62 Expenditure	(4) 1962/63 Allocation	(5) 1962/63 Expenditure	(6) 1963/64 Budget Allocation	Total (3) + (5)
Airports	14.25	0.38	0.34	0.40	0.64	3.60	0.98
Roads and Streets	24.25	4.42	4.74	4.20	3.49	3.60	8.23
Sewers and Drainage	16.50	2.40	1.89	1.70	1.71	2.60	3.60
Housing	14.63	1.05	0.84	0.35	0.35	1.95	1.19
Hospitals and Other Public Health Facilities	16.45	1.81	0.99	1.39	0.90	1.67	1.89
Schools and Other Education Facilities	29.00	1.74	1.05	4.54	4.16	9.95	5.21
Ports	5.63	1.26	0.93	0.58	0.58	1.25	1.51
Government Buildings	17.54	6.20	4.66	3.99	3.82	2.80	8.48
Electricity and Water[1]	n.a.	10.62	7.05	8.35	7.45	10.75	14.50
Miscellaneous	n.a.	2.50	3.85	4.55	3.70	3.90	7.55
Sub total (Capital)	138.25	32.38	26.34	30.05	26.80	42.07	53.14
Current Expenditures of PWD	—	5.77	9.33	9.50	8.58	8.28	17.91
Total	138.25	38.15	35.67	39.55	35.38	50.35	71.05

[1] Capital expenditures only.

Source: Ministries of Public Works, Electricity and Water, and Finance and Industry.

175

TABLE VIII: Cost of Distilled Water in Fils per 1,000 Gallons

	Actual Cost at 4,148,000 Gallons per Day (1962/63 Av.)	Estimated Cost at 6,000,000 Gallons per Day (Installed Capacity)	Estimated Cost In Original Plant "A" at Installed Capacity of 1,000,000 Gallons per Day	Estimated Cost in Newest Plant "E" at Installed Capacity of 2,000,000 Gallons per Day
Depreciation of Plant	331	229	850	114
	331	229	850	114
Operation				
Salaries and Wages—Evaporator Staff	47	33	95	23
—Boiler Staff	27	19	41	15
Fuel, Lubricants, Chemicals	69	58	52	57
Electricity	34	29	2	12
	177	139	190	107
Maintenance				
Salaries and Wages	52	36	176	15
Salaries, Wages, Materials—Boiler Maintenance	7	5	10	4
Materials	35	24	72	8
Workshop Services	10	7	47	1
	104	72	305	28
Overheads				
General Expenses, Technical, Administration, Accounts and General Control	48	33	103	20
	48	33	103	20
Total	660	473	1,448	269
	(185¢)	(132¢)	(406¢)	(75¢)

Source: Ministry of Power and Water.

176

TABLE IX: Credit Bank: Summary of Industrial Applications to October 21, 1963

(All in Kuwait Dinars)

	No. of Applications	Applied for	Approved		Rejected		Withdrawn or Postponed		Paid to Oct. 21, 1963	
Ironworks	5	15,500	(2)	6,500	(1)	500	(2)	7,500	(2)	4,590
Garages	20	552,850	(8)	32,000	(3)	203,300	(10)	312,550	(3)	15,500
Carpenters	8	138,500	(5)	95,800		—	(3)	7,500	(3)	69,920
Cold Stores	5	87,500	(4)	60,000		—		—	(3)	29,000
Printing	4	121,595	(2)	40,000		—	(2)	71,595	(1)	19,500
Tire Retreading	1	4,500	(1)	4,500		—		—	(1)	4,500
Laundries	4	8,750	(1)	250		—	(3)	8,000	(1)	250
Engineering and Contracting	4	345,000	(2)	150,000	(1)	—		—	(2)	100,000
Soap	2	380,000		—		—	(2)	380,000		—
Marble, Tiles and Mosaics	3	57,000	(1)	20,000	(2)	37,000		—		—
Mineral Water	2	135,000		—	(1)	65,000	(1)	70,000		—
Asbestos Pipe	1	200,000	(1)	200,000		—		—	(1)	150,000
Food and Drink	2	30,000	(1)	3,000	(1)	20,000		—	(1)	3,000
Sundries	10	10,050	(2)	2,750		—	(9)	8,050	(1)	500
	71	2,086,245	(30)	614,800	(9)	325,800	(32)	865,195	(19)	396,760

Note: Numbers in brackets denote number of projects.
Source: Credit Bank.

TABLE X: Yields and Water Requirements of Vegetables

Crop	Yield in Long Tons per Acre	Retail Price of Product in Dinars per Ton	Irrigation Water Required in 1,000 Gallons per Acre per Crop	Retail Value of Product in Dinars per 1,000 Gallons of Water
Snake Cucumber (Spring)	16.52	83	608	2.25
Cabbage	13.60	168	1,094	2.09
Cauliflower	19.20	101	962	2.02
Carrots	13.20	168	1,458	1.52
Tomatoes	18.40	168	2,025	1.52
Snake Cucumber (Autumn)	16.52	83	1,013	1.35
Endive	13.00	143	1,458	1.28
Lettuce	13.40	83	962	1.16
Swiss Chard	29.04	83	2,268	1.06
Spinach	14.95	125	1,782	1.05
Turnips	13.20	83	1,135	0.96
Watermelons (Spring)	6.48	58	648	0.58
Beets	10.08	83	1,457	0.57
Cucumber	2.83	168	892	0.53
Onions	3.92	83	811	0.40
Melons (Spring)	5.33	58	811	0.38
Peas	2.50	168	1,135	0.37
Water Melons (Autumn)	6.48	58	1,215	0.31
Melons (Autumn)	5.33	58	1,620	0.19
Okra	4.00	251	6,080	0.17

Source: Government Experimental Farm.

TABLE XI: Kuwaitis and Non-Kuwaitis in the Graded Permanent Posts

Group and Grade	All Ministries except Armed Forces				
	Officials and Employees July 31, 1963			Percentage to Total	
	Total	Kuwaitis	Non-Kuwaitis	Kuwaitis	Non-Kuwaitis
Group I					
Distinguished A	3	3	—	100	—
Distinguished B	1	1	—	100	—
Under Secretary	20	18	2	90	10
Asst. Under Secretary	44	35	9	80	20
Group II					
Grade I	83	32	51	39	61
Grade II	201	76	125	38	62
Grade III	612	188	424	31	69
Grade IV	1,255	391	864	31	69
Grade III					
Grade I	2,339	810	1,529	35	65
Grade II	3,753	1,346	2,407	36	64
Grade III	6,141	2,263	3,878	37	63
Grade IV	7,621	6,101	1,520	81	19
Group IV					
Grade I	3,126	1,294	1,832	41	59
Grade II	3,658	1,787	1,871	49	51
Grade III	7,487	2,341	5,146	31	69
Officials					
Group I–III	22,073	11,264	10,809	51	49
Officials & Employees					
Group I–IV	36,344	16,686	19,658	45	55

TABLE XII: Schedules of Salaries and Grades

Grade	Monthly Salary	Annual Increment	Minimum Period to be Completed in the Grade
	Schedule No. 1 *Superior Posts*		
Distinguished Grade "A"	KD 400	Flat rate	No time limit
Distinguished Grade "B"	KD 350	Flat rate	No time limit
Under Secretary	KD 330	Flat rate	No time limit
Asst. Under Secretary	KD 300	Flat rate	No time limit
	Schedule No. 2 *Senior Posts*		
Grade I	From KD 219.375 to 275.625	KD 11.250	No time limit
Grade II	KD 181.875 to 219.375	KD 7.500	2 years
Grade III	KD 148.125 to 181.875	KD 6.750	3 years
Grade IV	KD 120.000 to 148.125	KD 5.625	3 years
	Schedule No. 3 *Intermediate Posts*		
Grade I	From KD 87.375 to 123.375	KD 4.500	—
Grade II	KD 68.625 to 87.375	KD 3.750	3 years
Grade III	KD 51.750 to 68.625	KD 3.375	4 years
Grade IV	KD 33.750 to 51.750	KD 3.000	4 years
	Schedule No. 4 *Employees*		
Grade I	From KD 41.250 to 57.000	KD 2.650	—
Grade II	KD 30.000 to 41.250	KD 2.250	4 years
Grade III	KD 18.750 to 30.000	KD 1.875	4 years

TABLE XIII: Notified Deaths, Kuwait 1962, by Age and Cause

Disease Groups	Age Groups							
	Below 1 yr.	1–5	5–10	10–15	15–30	30–50	50 and Over	Total
Infectious Diseases	3	4		1	10	4	12	34
Tumors		2	1		4	11	39	57
Blood Diseases	6	7	4	1	3	9	13	43
Diseases of the Circulatory System	36	16	6	1	37	57	112	265
Diseases of the Nervous System	25	10	7	4	17	21	21	105
Diseases of the Respiratory System	140	47	11	4	57	51	72	382
Diseases of the Gastro-Intestinal Tract	136	25	1		12	14	8	196
Diseases of the Genito-Urinary System	4	1		1	4	8	10	28
Senility and Similar Conditions						4	77	81
Poisoning	3	2	3	1	19	16	13	57
Maldevelopment	102	1						103
Diseases of the Locomotor System	5	1	2		10	7	2	27
Other Causes	22	16	14	4	61	60	19	196
Total	482	132	49	17	234	262	398	1,574

TABLE XIV: Notified Cases of Infectious Diseases During 1962

Infectious Diseases	Age Groups								Total
	Below 1 Yr.	1-5	5-10	10-15	15-30	30-50	50 and Over	Not Stated	
Cerebrospinal Fever	—	—	1	—	—	—	—	3	4
Scarlet Fever	—	1	2	—	1	—	—	1	5
Acute Poliomyelitis	6	20	4	1	1	—	1	6	39
Infectious Hepatitis	2	14	9	2	12	5	—	2	46
German Measles	—	—	—	—	—	—	—	—	—
Typhoid	1	6	12	30	70	11	1	9	140
Para-Typhoid	11	6	4	3	8	2	1	5	40
Diphtheria	5	39	29	7	5	1	—	19	105
Measles	171	543	125	34	53	3	—	88	1,017
Whooping Cough	12	77	32	5	6	—	—	14	146
Parotitis (Mumps)	6	109	338	111	105	17	—	49	735
Leprosy	—	—	—	3	6	3	—	1	13
Malaria	—	—	—	—	4	2	—	18	24
Tetanus	4	1	1	1	1	—	—	1	9
Pulmonary Tuberculosis	7	40	33	55	381	212	72	37	837
Chickenpox	89	323	430	153	244	93	6	212	1,550
Influenza	—	—	4	2	17	12	—	9	44
Overp Sepsis	—	—	—	—	—	—	—	1	1
Bacillary and Amoebic Dysentery	3	16	5	3	11	3	4	504	549

TABLE XV: Scholarship Students in the Year 1963/64

College	Boys	Girls	Per Cent of Total
Arts	40	48	16.2
Commerce	28	1	1.7
Law	8	1	5.3
Economics and Political Science	18	2	3.7
Medicine	74	4	14.4
Dentistry	6	2	1.5
Pharmacy	4	—	0.7
Laboratory Technician	12	—	2.2
X-Ray	4	—	0.7
Physiotherapy	2	—	0.4
Science	1	—	0.2
Engineering	153	—	27.2
Arabic Language	25	—	4.6
Islamic Law	11	—	2.0
Technical Studies	14	—	2.6
Social Services	2	—	0.4
Physical Education	13	—	4.8
Health Studies	2	—	0.4
Police	6	—	1.1
Study for the Blind	2	—	0.4
Teachers Training	37	—	6.8
Artistic Education	3	—	0.7
Geology	15	—	2.8
Mathematics	5	—	0.9
Commercial Naval Studies	2	—	0.4
Total	487	56	100.0

Source: Ministry of Education.

TABLE XVI: Students and Classes by Type of School

	STUDENTS		
Type	1962/63	1963/64	Percentage Increase
Kindergartens	6,614	7,998	21
Primary	33,895	39,808	17
Intermediate	13,728	17,130	25
Secondary	3,519	4,199	19
Vocational	946	578	—39
Special Schools	849	1,096	29
Total	59,551	70,809	19
	CLASSES		
Type	1962/63	1963/64	Percentage Increase
Kindergartens	192	236	23
Primary	928	1,080	16
Intermediate	446	523	17
Secondary	109	142	30
Vocational	101	53	—48
Special Schools	68	86	26
Total	1,844	2,120	15

TABLE XVII: School Construction

Category of School	Constructed to End of 1960/61	Constructed to End of 1961/62	Constructed to End of 1962/63	Constructed to End of 1963/64	To be Constructed to End of 1964/65	To Be Constructed to End of 1965/66
Kindergarten	5	4		6		9
Primary	12	5	2	9	2	6
Intermediate	1			2	8	
Secondary		1	1	1	1	5
Teacher Training						
Technical						
Commercial				1		
Retarded and Handicapped				1		
Religious						
Total	18	10	3	20	11	20

Source: Ministry of Education.

185

TABLE XVIII: Kuwait Share Companies

Name of Company	Government Share (Percentage)	Capital in KD
With Government Equity Participation		
Kuwait Airways	100	398,310[a]
Kuwait National Petroleum [b]	60	7,500,000
National Industries	51	1,500,000
Petrochemicals	40	16,000,000
Flour Mills	50	2,000,000
Kuwait Investments	50	15,000,000
Kuwait Hotels	25	2,000,000
Kuwait Transport	50	2,000,000
Kuwait Navigation	50	—
Kuwait Asbestos	$38\frac{1}{4}$ [c]	360,000[d]
With Private Equity Participation Only		
Kuwait Oil Tanker		5,751,540
Kuwait Cinema		654,105
Kuwait Insurance		375,000
Commercial Bank of Kuwait		1,500,000
Gulf Bank		1,800,000
Gulf Insurance		800,000
National Insurance		1,000,000
National Bank of Kuwait		1,965,000
Kuwait National Fisheries		1,000,000
Kuwait Limestone		10,000
Kuwait Aviation Fueling		14,700
Vegetables and Fruit		—[e]

[a] Before nationalization.

[b] The Kuwait National Petroleum Co., capitalized at $21,000,000 was organized in the middle of 1960 for the purpose of engaging in the oil industry at home and abroad. The Government subscribed for 60 per cent of the shares and the balance was offered to Kuwaiti nationals. In June 1961, the Kuwait National Company bought from the Kuwait Oil Company its oil-products distribution facilities. On October 21, 1962, the Government approved the Kuwait National Petroleum Co.'s application for a concession to prospect for oil in the areas relinquished in May by the Kuwait Oil Company; the terms of the concession were to be negotiated.

[c] But actual control rests with the Government since 75 per cent of the Asbestos Company stock is owned by National Industries Company in which the Government has a 51 per cent interest.

[d] Not yet registered.

[e] Not yet registered.

TABLE XIX: Analysis of Typical Gas from Burgan Field

(Molecular Percentage*)

	Separator at 400 lbs./sq.in.	Separator at 40 lbs./sq.in.	Atmospheric Gas
Methane	74.3	52.9	20.3
Ethane	14.0	20.0	22.2
Propane	5.8	13.2	27.8
Butane	2.0	6.3	17.2
Pentane	0.7	2.4	6.4
Hexane and Heavier	0.2	0.9	1.8
Hydrogen Sulphide	0.1	0.4	0.4
Carbon Dioxide, Oxygen, Nitrogen	2.9	3.9	3.9
Total	100.0	100.0	100.0
Gross Calorific Value (BTU/FI3)	1,260	1,600	2,260

* Approximately by volume.